ROBOTICS WITH RASPBERRY PI: BUILD YOUR FIRST ROBOT

A Hands-on Guide to Coding, Assembling, and Controlling Robots

THOMPSON CARTER

TABLE OF CONTENTS

INTRODUCTION

ROBOTICS WITH RASPBERRY PI: BUILD YOUR FIRST ROBOT

Welcome to *Robotics with Raspberry Pi: Build Your First Robot*, a comprehensive, hands-on guide that will take you from understanding the basics of robotics and Raspberry Pi to creating a fully functional robot that you can control, expand, and showcase. Whether you're a student, hobbyist, or technology enthusiast, this book is designed to provide a jargon-free, practical approach to robotics, making complex concepts accessible and enjoyable. By the end of this journey, you'll not only have a working robot but also a strong foundation in robotics, programming, and engineering principles that will serve you well in future projects.

Why Robotics with Raspberry Pi?

The world of robotics combines elements from a broad spectrum of fields, including mechanical engineering, electronics, programming, and artificial intelligence. Robotics offers a unique opportunity to see theory come to life as machines respond to code and interact with their environment. The Raspberry Pi, with its powerful yet affordable computing capabilities, has revolutionized robotics education by making these technologies accessible to a wide audience. Here are some of the reasons why building robots with the Raspberry Pi is particularly compelling:

1. **Affordability**: Raspberry Pi is an economical yet powerful platform, costing a fraction of what traditional robotics setups require.

2. **Versatility**: Equipped with GPIO (General Purpose Input/Output) pins, the Raspberry Pi can interface with a wide variety of sensors, motors, and devices, making it ideal for building robots that interact with the physical world.

3. **Open Source Community**: Raspberry Pi's open-source ecosystem has led to a vast library of resources, guides, and forums. This strong community makes it easy to find help, tutorials, and inspiration for your projects.

4. **Educational Value**: Robotics with Raspberry Pi introduces foundational concepts in programming, electronics, and AI in a way that is approachable yet rigorous, equipping you with skills that are in high demand in today's technology-driven world.

In this book, we'll leverage these strengths to create a robot that is not only functional but can also be expanded with advanced features. With step-by-step guidance and practical examples, you'll learn how to turn ideas into reality.

What You'll Learn

This book is structured to guide you from the basics to more advanced robotics concepts. Each chapter builds on the previous one, providing a progressive learning experience with hands-on projects. Here's a preview of what you'll learn:

- **Setting Up and Programming Raspberry Pi**: You'll start with Raspberry Pi basics, including how to set up the device, navigate its operating system, and write basic programs in Python, a user-friendly language that is perfect for beginners but powerful enough for complex applications.

- **Understanding Electronics and Sensors**: Building a robot involves more than just writing code; it requires a fundamental understanding of how electronic components work. We'll cover essential components like resistors, capacitors, LEDs, and basic circuits, followed by an exploration of sensors used in robotics to detect light, distance, temperature, and motion.

- **Robot Construction and Motor Control**: You'll learn to build a basic chassis and wire up motors to give your robot mobility. Through hands-on projects, you'll program motor controls, enabling the robot to move forward, backward, and turn. By understanding how to control motors accurately, you'll have the basis for navigation and autonomous movement.

- **Implementing Interaction and Control**: Interaction is key to robotics. In later chapters, you'll incorporate sensors that allow your robot to respond to its environment. From simple collision avoidance to line-following capabilities, these projects will show you how to program behaviors that make your robot appear smart and reactive.

- **Advanced Control Options**: Once your robot is operational, you'll explore options for remote and autonomous control. We'll cover wireless control using Wi-Fi, including how to set up a web-based control interface, as well as voice commands, allowing you to interact with your robot hands-free.

- **Artificial Intelligence and Computer Vision**: Robotics and AI are becoming increasingly intertwined. We'll introduce basic machine learning concepts and apply them to robotics through object detection and color tracking. This section will also cover real-time image processing using OpenCV, adding a vision-based dimension to your robot's capabilities.

- **Testing, Debugging, and Optimization**: Building a reliable robot requires thorough testing and optimization. You'll learn techniques for debugging hardware and software, refining your code, calibrating sensors, and improving motor accuracy. These practices ensure your robot operates smoothly and predictably, whether it's for a demonstration or practical use.

- **Showcasing and Expanding Your Project**: Finally, you'll learn how to showcase your completed robot, document your process, and expand your project with advanced features such as SLAM (Simultaneous Localization and Mapping) and IoT (Internet of Things) connectivity. You'll be equipped to present your work effectively and continue building upon it.

Who This Book is For

This book is designed for anyone interested in robotics, whether you're a complete beginner, a student, or an enthusiast with some background in programming or electronics. While a basic familiarity with programming will be helpful, no prior experience in robotics is required. The step-by-step instructions, detailed explanations, and real-world examples make this book accessible to learners of all levels.

The projects in this book are versatile enough to fit a variety of interests and learning goals. You might be a high school student exploring robotics as a potential career path, an engineering student looking for a practical application of your studies, or a hobbyist excited to dive into a new challenge. By the end of this book, you'll be equipped with the skills to build, modify, and expand your own robots.

How to Use This Book

The chapters in this book are designed to be sequential, each one building on the knowledge from previous chapters. As you progress, you'll gain the skills to construct and program a robot from scratch, culminating in a fully functional, interactive robot that you can demonstrate or expand further. Here's how to approach this book:

1. **Follow the Chapters in Order**: Each chapter builds on concepts introduced earlier, so it's best to progress through the book in sequence, especially if you're new to robotics.

2. **Complete the Hands-On Projects**: Practical experience is essential in robotics. Each chapter contains a hands-on project that reinforces the concepts covered. These projects allow you to apply what you've learned and troubleshoot along the way, which is a crucial part of the learning process.

3. **Experiment and Customize**: Feel free to modify and experiment with the projects in this book. Robotics is all about creativity and problem-solving, so don't hesitate to try new ideas or expand on the projects with your own modifications.

4. **Use as a Reference Guide**: Once you've completed the book, it can serve as a reference for future robotics projects. You'll have a set of core skills that you can apply to other Raspberry Pi or electronics projects.

The Future of Robotics with Raspberry Pi

The Raspberry Pi has become an educational and prototyping powerhouse, inspiring countless projects across industries, from automation and agriculture to artificial intelligence and healthcare. As more affordable and powerful models are introduced, the possibilities for robotics projects continue to expand.

This book is just the beginning. By gaining hands-on experience with Raspberry Pi robotics, you're opening the door to a vast world of possibilities. With the skills you acquire here, you'll be able to create robots that are increasingly autonomous, responsive, and intelligent. Whether you're interested in building robots for fun, for competition, or even for professional applications, the foundation you develop here will serve as a springboard for your future projects.

Robotics is an immensely rewarding field that combines the thrill of creation with the satisfaction of problem-solving. Building your own robot is a journey that teaches you not only technical skills but also patience, creativity, and resilience. Throughout this book, you'll make mistakes, solve problems, and see your robot come to life, piece by piece. By the end, you'll have a robot that is uniquely yours, along with a strong foundation in robotics and a toolkit of skills that will serve you well in countless future projects.

So, let's get started. Grab your Raspberry Pi, gather your components, and prepare to dive into the fascinating world of robotics. Your journey to building, programming, and understanding robots begins now!

Chapter 1: Introduction to Robotics and Raspberry Pi

Welcome to the world of robotics with Raspberry Pi! This chapter introduces the fundamental concepts of robotics, explores its real-world applications, and discusses why the Raspberry Pi is an ideal platform for beginners and hobbyists alike to dive into robotics. We'll conclude with a high-level roadmap of what you'll learn throughout this book, setting clear goals and expectations as we embark on the journey to building your first robot.

Overview of Robotics and Its Applications in the Real World
What is Robotics?

Robotics is the intersection of engineering, computer science, and artificial intelligence to create machines (robots) capable of performing tasks autonomously or semi-autonomously. A robot typically consists of sensors to perceive its environment, actuators (like motors) to interact with its surroundings, a processing unit (such as a microcontroller or computer) to make decisions, and often, some form of software to control these elements.

Robots can be found in various fields, including:

- **Manufacturing**: Robots in factories help automate repetitive tasks, increasing efficiency and safety by taking over physically demanding jobs.
- **Healthcare**: Robots assist in surgery, patient care, and therapy. Surgical robots, for example, provide precision and control beyond human capabilities.
- **Exploration**: Robots play a significant role in space and underwater exploration. Rovers, such as NASA's Mars rovers, are designed to explore distant planets autonomously.
- **Agriculture**: Robots in farming help with planting, harvesting, and monitoring crops, allowing for sustainable and precision agriculture.
- **Everyday Life**: Robots are becoming more common in our homes, from robot vacuum cleaners to personal assistant robots.

These examples illustrate how robotics is transforming industries and impacting daily life, making it an exciting field to explore.

Key Components of a Robot

1. **Sensors**: Gather information from the environment (e.g., distance sensors, cameras, microphones).
2. **Actuators**: Control the robot's movement and interaction with the physical world (e.g., motors, servos).
3. **Processor**: The "brain" of the robot, which processes information and makes decisions (e.g., microcontrollers, single-board computers like the Raspberry Pi).
4. **Software**: Programs that control the robot's behavior, enabling it to respond to the environment.

By building your own robot with Raspberry Pi, you'll gain experience with all these components and learn how they interact to create a functional machine.

Why Raspberry Pi is Ideal for Robotics Projects

The Raspberry Pi, a small yet powerful single-board computer, is widely regarded as one of the best platforms for beginner and intermediate robotics projects. Here's why it's perfect for building your first robot:

1. **Affordable and Accessible**: Raspberry Pi boards are low-cost and widely available, making them an excellent choice for educational and hobbyist projects.

2. **Computational Power**: Unlike simple microcontrollers (e.g., Arduino), the Raspberry Pi runs a full operating system and supports complex software applications, allowing you to use Python, computer vision, and even machine learning models on your robot.

3. **Versatile I/O**: Raspberry Pi boards come equipped with a set of General Purpose Input/Output (GPIO) pins, enabling you to connect sensors, motors, and other components directly. This makes it easy to integrate a variety of electronic components into your robot.

4. **Operating System and Software Ecosystem**: Raspberry Pi OS (formerly Raspbian) is a full-fledged operating system based on Linux, with support for Python, C++, and many other programming languages. It includes a robust set of tools, libraries, and documentation specifically tailored for hardware projects.

5. **Community and Support**: The Raspberry Pi has a large community of enthusiasts, developers, and educators who create guides, tutorials, and projects. This rich ecosystem of resources helps you troubleshoot issues and find inspiration for building new projects.

6. **Portability and Scalability**: A Raspberry Pi can power various robotics projects, from simple mobile robots to complex systems with cameras, sensors, and machine learning models. This scalability allows beginners to start small and build increasingly advanced robots.

In summary, the Raspberry Pi is not only affordable and powerful but also easy to learn, making it an ideal choice for building and programming your first robot.

Setting Goals for the Book and a High-Level Roadmap of What You'll Learn

The goal of this book is to guide you step-by-step through building and programming a robot with a Raspberry Pi. By the end of the book, you will have constructed a robot that can move, sense its environment, avoid obstacles, follow lines, and more. You'll learn the basics of robotics and gain practical experience with programming, electronics, and sensors, equipping you with the foundational skills to pursue more advanced robotics projects.

What You'll Learn in Each Section

The book is structured to take you from the basics of Raspberry Pi and Python programming to building your own fully functional robot. Here's a roadmap of the topics we'll cover:

1. **Getting Started with Raspberry Pi and Python**:

> o Chapters 2-3 will introduce you to the Raspberry Pi and Python programming. You'll set up your development environment, learn basic Python syntax, and write your first program.

2. **Understanding Electronics and GPIO Programming**:

> o Chapters 4-5 cover the basics of electronics, including how to build circuits and connect sensors and actuators to the Raspberry Pi's GPIO pins.

3. **Building and Powering Your Robot**:

> o Chapters 6-8 introduce motors, motor drivers, and assembling your robot chassis. You'll learn how to control your robot's movement and set up a reliable power source.

4. **Sensors and Interaction with the Environment**:

> o Chapters 9-12 focus on adding sensors to your robot. You'll learn how to make your robot "see" and "feel" its surroundings by integrating sensors like ultrasonic distance sensors and configuring them for obstacle avoidance.

5. **Expanding Control Options**:

> o Chapters 10-11 explore different ways to control your robot, including remote control via Bluetooth and programming control loops to make your robot move autonomously.

6. **Building More Advanced Functionalities**:

o Chapters 13-20 introduce advanced concepts, such as line-following, camera integration, object detection, machine learning, voice control, and web-based control. Each chapter builds a specific capability, such as having your robot follow a line or recognize objects.

7. **Testing, Debugging, and Optimization**:

o Chapter 21 teaches you how to troubleshoot, optimize, and improve your robot's performance, covering common issues and debugging tips.

8. **Showcasing and Expanding Your Robot**:

o In Chapter 22, you'll learn how to prepare your robot for demonstrations and explore ideas for adding new features and expanding your project.

Throughout the book, you'll find hands-on projects and real-world examples, helping you understand each concept by applying it to a working robot. By the end of each chapter, you'll have built a new feature or learned a new skill that directly contributes to your final project.

What You'll Achieve by the End of the Book

By following the steps and completing the exercises in this book, you will:

- **Build a Functional Robot**: You'll assemble a mobile robot that can move, sense its surroundings, and respond to commands. Each chapter adds a layer of functionality, from basic movement to advanced tasks like object detection and navigation.

- **Gain Practical Programming and Electronics Skills**: This book not only teaches robotics but also provides a solid foundation in Python programming and basic electronics. You'll learn how to connect and control components like motors, LEDs, sensors, and more.

- **Understand Core Robotics Concepts**: You'll become familiar with robotics fundamentals, such as control loops, obstacle avoidance, sensor integration, and object tracking, giving you the knowledge to build increasingly complex robots in the future.

- **Learn to Troubleshoot and Optimize**: Robotics projects often involve troubleshooting, and you'll gain valuable skills in debugging hardware and software, optimizing performance, and solving common robotics challenges.

- **Create a Portfolio Project**: Building a robot from scratch is a rewarding experience and can serve as a valuable addition to your portfolio, showcasing your technical and creative abilities.

Robotics with Raspberry Pi offers a unique and exciting way to learn programming, electronics, and engineering concepts. This book is designed to be accessible to beginners, with each chapter building on the last in a logical progression. Whether you're interested in robotics as a hobby, looking to develop skills for a career, or simply eager to bring your ideas to life, this book will provide you with the foundational knowledge and practical experience needed to succeed.

So, let's get started on this journey! With patience, creativity, and determination, you'll soon have a fully functional robot that you've built and programmed yourself. Welcome to the world of robotics with Raspberry Pi!

CHAPTER 2: GETTING STARTED WITH RASPBERRY PI

In this chapter, we'll guide you through the initial setup of your Raspberry Pi, an affordable yet powerful single-board computer that serves as the "brain" of your robot. From choosing the right model to setting up the software and getting familiar with basic commands, we'll cover everything you need to get your Raspberry Pi ready for robotics.

Choosing a Raspberry Pi Model and Setting Up the Hardware

The Raspberry Pi family includes various models, each with different capabilities. For robotics projects, here are some models to consider:

1. **Raspberry Pi 4 Model B**: The most powerful option, with multiple RAM options (2GB, 4GB, and 8GB). It has a quad-core CPU, dual HDMI ports, USB 3.0, and more GPIO pins, making it suitable for robotics and more advanced tasks, including AI and image processing.
2. **Raspberry Pi 3 Model B+**: A solid choice for robotics. It has built-in Wi-Fi and Bluetooth, making it easy to connect sensors and peripherals wirelessly.
3. **Raspberry Pi Zero W**: A more compact and budget-friendly option with built-in Wi-Fi and Bluetooth. It's ideal for simpler robots or projects where space is a priority, but it may struggle with heavy processing tasks.

For most robotics projects, the **Raspberry Pi 4 Model B** is recommended because it has the processing power needed for more complex operations like camera input or machine learning.

Essential Hardware for Setup To set up your Raspberry Pi, you'll need:

- **Raspberry Pi board** (model of your choice)
- **MicroSD card** (16GB or more, preferably Class 10 for speed)

- **Power supply** (5V, 3A for Raspberry Pi 4)
- **HDMI cable** (micro-HDMI for Raspberry Pi 4, mini-HDMI for Raspberry Pi Zero)
- **Monitor and keyboard/mouse** (for initial setup; can use remote access later)
- **USB card reader** (if your computer doesn't have an SD card slot)

Installing Raspberry Pi OS and Setting Up Essential Software Tools

Once you have your hardware ready, it's time to install the operating system and prepare the software environment. Raspberry Pi OS (formerly Raspbian) is a Linux-based operating system optimized for the Raspberry Pi. It provides a full desktop environment, tools, and libraries tailored for programming and hardware projects.

Step 1: Download Raspberry Pi OS

1. Visit the Raspberry Pi Downloads page and download the **Raspberry Pi Imager** tool.
2. Insert your microSD card into your computer, then open Raspberry Pi Imager.
3. Select **Choose OS**, then select **Raspberry Pi OS (32-bit)** for general use.
4. Click **Choose Storage** and select your SD card.

5. Click **Write** to install the OS onto the microSD card. This process may take a few minutes.

Step 2: Booting Up Raspberry Pi

1. Insert the microSD card into the Raspberry Pi.
2. Connect the monitor, keyboard, and mouse.
3. Plug in the power supply to power on the Raspberry Pi.
4. The Raspberry Pi OS setup screen will appear. Follow the on-screen instructions to set up your language, time zone, and Wi-Fi (if applicable).
5. Update the system when prompted to ensure you have the latest software and security patches.

Step 3: Setting Up Essential Software Tools

After setting up Raspberry Pi OS, you'll need to install some essential tools and libraries for robotics and programming:

- **Python**: Raspberry Pi OS comes with Python pre-installed, as it's the primary language for Raspberry Pi projects. Verify the installation by opening the Terminal and typing python3 --version.
- **GPIO Library**: The RPi.GPIO library allows you to interact with the Raspberry Pi's GPIO pins. This library should be pre-installed, but you can install or update it with:

bash

Copy code

sudo apt update

sudo apt install python3-rpi.gpio

Other Useful Tools

- **VNC (Virtual Network Computing)**: Allows you to control your Raspberry Pi remotely from another computer. Enable it in the Raspberry Pi configuration menu.
- **Visual Studio Code**: A powerful code editor that works well with Python and other languages. You can install it with:

bash

sudo apt update

sudo apt install code -y

Introduction to Basic Linux Commands and Navigating the Raspberry Pi

With Raspberry Pi OS installed, the Terminal (command line) is a powerful tool you'll use frequently for robotics projects. Here's a quick introduction to essential Linux commands to help you navigate and manage files on your Raspberry Pi.

Basic Commands for File Management and Navigation

1. **Checking Your Location**: Use pwd (print working directory) to see your current location in the file system.

bash
pwd

2. **Listing Files**: Use ls to list files and directories in your current location.

bash
ls

3. **Changing Directories**: Use cd to change directories.
   - Go to a specific directory: cd directory_name
   - Go up one level: cd ..

bash
cd Documents

4. **Creating and Deleting Directories**:
   - Make a new directory with mkdir: mkdir my_folder
   - Remove a directory with rmdir: rmdir my_folder (use rm -r my_folder for non-empty directories)

5. **Creating and Editing Files**:
   - Create a new file with touch: touch my_file.txt
   - Use nano, a simple text editor, to edit files in the Terminal: nano my_file.txt

6. **Viewing and Editing Files**:
   - o To view the contents of a file: cat my_file.txt
   - o To edit a file with Nano, type nano filename, make your changes, then save by pressing **Ctrl + O** and exit with **Ctrl + X**.

Useful System Commands

1. **Updating and Upgrading Software**: Keep your software up-to-date with these commands:

   bash

   sudo apt update

   sudo apt upgrade

2. **Rebooting and Shutting Down**:
   - o Reboot: sudo reboot
   - o Shut down: sudo shutdown now

3. **Checking System Information**:
   - o Check CPU usage: top or htop
   - o Check disk usage: df -h
   - o Check IP address: hostname -I

Setting Up and Using GPIO Pins

1. **Checking GPIO Pin Layout**: You can refer to the official GPIO pin layout at the Raspberry Pi website or print it in the Terminal using:

bash

pinout

2. **Basic GPIO Commands**: Once you start working with GPIO pins, you'll use the GPIO library in Python to control them. A basic setup might look like this:

python
import RPi.GPIO as GPIO
GPIO.setmode(GPIO.BCM)   # Use BCM numbering for GPIO
GPIO.setup(18, GPIO.OUT) # Set pin 18 as an output
GPIO.output(18, GPIO.HIGH) # Turn on pin 18
GPIO.cleanup() # Clean up pins when done

In this chapter, we covered the essential steps to get your Raspberry Pi ready for robotics projects. From choosing the right Raspberry Pi model to installing Raspberry Pi OS and configuring necessary software, you've prepared the foundation for a successful robotics journey. We also introduced basic Linux commands, which will be invaluable as you navigate the Raspberry Pi's file system and control its GPIO pins for hardware interaction.

By the end of this chapter, you should have a working Raspberry Pi set up with the necessary tools for programming and robotics. In the next chapter, we'll dive into Python programming essentials, preparing you to start writing scripts and controlling your robot's hardware components.

With your Raspberry Pi ready and these foundational skills in place, you're well-equipped to begin building your first robot!

CHAPTER 3: INTRODUCTION TO PYTHON FOR ROBOTICS

Python is the primary programming language used in Raspberry Pi robotics due to its simplicity, readability, and robust ecosystem of libraries that support hardware interaction and data processing. In this chapter, we'll introduce you to Python programming essentials, focusing on the syntax and structures necessary for robotics projects. By the end, you'll write and execute your first Python program on the Raspberry Pi, setting the stage for future chapters that delve into controlling hardware and adding functionality to your robot.

Why Python is the Preferred Language for Raspberry Pi Robotics

Python's popularity in the robotics community stems from several advantages:

1. **Ease of Use and Readability**: Python's syntax is clean and concise, making it accessible for beginners. With simple commands and a vast library ecosystem, Python enables you to focus on building functionality without getting bogged down by complex syntax.

2. **Extensive Library Support**: Python has a vast selection of libraries that make it easy to interface with hardware components. For Raspberry Pi projects, libraries like RPi.GPIO and gpiozero allow you to control GPIO pins and interact with sensors, motors, and other electronic components directly.

3. **Compatibility with Advanced Tools**: Python's compatibility with powerful libraries for robotics, such as

OpenCV for image processing and TensorFlow for machine learning, means you can use Python to integrate advanced functionalities into your robot.

4. **Community and Documentation**: Python's widespread use in the Raspberry Pi and robotics communities means there are countless tutorials, resources, and support forums to help you troubleshoot issues and learn new skills.

Python's flexibility and community support make it an ideal choice for building, testing, and expanding robotics projects on the Raspberry Pi.

Basic Python Syntax: Variables, Loops, Functions, and Modules

Before diving into hardware control, let's go over some Python basics. If you're new to programming, this section will provide a foundation for understanding Python's syntax and structure. If you already have some experience, consider this a quick refresher.

1. Variables

In Python, variables store data values. You can assign a value to a variable without declaring its type explicitly. Python determines the type based on the assigned value.

Example:

python
```
robot_speed = 10  # Integer
```

robot_name = "PiBot" # String

battery_level = 80.5 # Float

2. Data Types

Python has several basic data types commonly used in robotics:

- **Integers** (int): Whole numbers, e.g., 10, -3
- **Floats** (float): Numbers with decimal points, e.g., 4.5, 3.14
- **Strings** (str): Text data, e.g., "Hello, World!"
- **Booleans** (bool): True or False values, e.g., True, False

Example:

python

is_robot_active = True

distance_to_object = 15.75

3. Operators

Operators allow you to perform operations on variables and values. Common operators include:

- **Arithmetic Operators**: +, -, *, /, // (floor division), % (modulus)
- **Comparison Operators**: ==, !=, >, <, >=, <=
- **Logical Operators**: and, or, not

Example:

python

```python
speed = 20
time = 5
distance = speed * time  # Multiplication: distance will be 100
```

4. Conditional Statements

Conditional statements allow your code to make decisions. In Python, if, elif, and else are used to execute code based on conditions.

Example:

```python
python
battery_level = 60

if battery_level > 50:
    print("Battery level is sufficient.")
elif battery_level > 20:
    print("Battery level is low.")
else:
    print("Battery is critical. Please charge.")
```

5. Loops

Loops allow you to execute a block of code multiple times. There are two primary loop types in Python:

- **For Loop**: Often used to iterate over a range or list.

    python

```
for i in range(5):
    print("Loop iteration:", i)
```

- **While Loop**: Runs as long as a condition is true.

```python
battery_level = 100
while battery_level > 0:
    print("Battery level:", battery_level)
    battery_level -= 10
```

6. Functions

Functions allow you to encapsulate code in reusable blocks. Define a function using the def keyword and call it by its name.

Example:

```python
def greet_robot(name):
    print(f"Hello, {name}! Ready for action?")


greet_robot("PiBot")
```

7. Modules and Libraries

A module is a file containing Python code, usually functions or classes. You can import modules to use existing functionality, which helps keep your code organized and efficient.

Example:

python
import math

distance = math.sqrt(16) # Using the sqrt function from the math module
print("Square root of 16 is:", distance)

Writing and Running Your First Python Program on the Raspberry Pi

With the basics of Python syntax covered, let's write a simple program to get familiar with the process of creating, saving, and executing Python code on the Raspberry Pi.

Step 1: Open a Text Editor

1. Open **Terminal** on your Raspberry Pi.
2. Use the nano text editor, which is pre-installed on Raspberry Pi OS, to create a new Python file.

   bash
   nano hello_robot.py

Step 2: Write Your Python Code

Inside the nano editor, type the following Python code. This program will ask for the robot's name and display a greeting.

python

hello_robot.py

robot_name = input("Enter your robot's name: ")

print(f"Hello, {robot_name}! Let's start coding.")

Here's a breakdown of what this code does:

- input() function prompts the user to enter the robot's name.
- print() function outputs a greeting that includes the name entered by the user.

Step 3: Save and Exit

1. Save the file by pressing **Ctrl + O**, then press **Enter** to confirm the filename.
2. Exit the editor by pressing **Ctrl + X**.

Step 4: Run Your Program

Back in the Terminal, run the program by typing:

bash

python3 hello_robot.py

When you run the code, it will prompt you to enter a robot name, then display the greeting.

Step 5: Try Modifying the Program

Now, let's expand on this simple program by adding a loop and a condition. Open the file again:

bash

nano hello_robot.py

Update the code to include a simple loop that repeats the greeting three times:

python

```python
# hello_robot.py
robot_name = input("Enter your robot's name: ")

for i in range(3):
    print(f"Hello, {robot_name}! Let's start coding.")
print("Goodbye!")
```

Save the file (**Ctrl + O**) and exit (**Ctrl + X**), then run the program again:

bash

python3 hello_robot.py

The program should now greet the robot three times before saying "Goodbye!"

In this chapter, you learned why Python is the preferred language for Raspberry Pi robotics and were introduced to essential Python syntax, including variables, loops, functions, and modules. You also created, saved, and ran your first Python program on the Raspberry Pi. These foundational skills will be essential as we progress through the book and begin building more complex code for controlling hardware and integrating robotics functionality.

By understanding Python's basic structures, you're now equipped to start programming your robot. In the next chapter, we'll introduce basic electronics and the components you'll be using in your robot, including how to connect these components to the Raspberry Pi.

Get ready to bring your robot to life!

CHAPTER 4: UNDERSTANDING THE BASICS OF ELECTRONICS

In this chapter, we'll introduce you to essential electronics concepts and components, including resistors, capacitors, LEDs, and how they work. We'll then explore using breadboards and jumper wires to build simple circuits, which will enable you to connect and control components through the Raspberry Pi's GPIO (General Purpose Input/Output) pins. Mastering these basics is crucial for building and expanding your robot.

Introduction to Key Electronic Components

Understanding a few fundamental components is essential for building circuits with the Raspberry Pi. Let's cover the basics of resistors, capacitors, and LEDs, which will be used throughout your robotics projects.

1. **Resistors**

   A resistor is a component that limits the flow of electric current in a circuit. Resistance is measured in ohms (Ω), and resistors are used to control the current flowing to sensitive components, such as LEDs, to prevent them from burning out.

   o **Color Bands**: Resistors have colored bands that indicate their resistance value. You can use an online calculator or a color chart to interpret the color bands.

- o **Example**: When using an LED, a resistor is often added in series with it to limit the current, preventing the LED from overheating.

2. **Capacitors**

Capacitors store and release electrical energy, which helps smooth out fluctuations in voltage. They are measured in farads (F) and come in various sizes and types.

- o **Polarized vs. Non-Polarized**: Some capacitors (like electrolytic capacitors) have polarity, meaning they have positive (+) and negative (−) leads and must be connected correctly in a circuit.
- o **Example**: Capacitors are often used in motor circuits to reduce electrical noise and prevent voltage spikes.

3. **LEDs (Light Emitting Diodes)**

LEDs are diodes that emit light when current flows through them. They're widely used as indicators in electronic projects because they're energy-efficient and easy to control.

- o **Polarity**: LEDs are polarized, meaning they have a positive (anode) and negative (cathode) side. The longer lead is typically the anode (+), and the shorter lead is the cathode (−).

- o **Current Limiting**: LEDs require resistors to limit the current, as too much current can damage them.

Quick Exercise: Get familiar with these components by identifying them physically. Try holding an LED, a resistor, and a capacitor, and notice their size and markings.

Working with Breadboards and Jumper Wires

Breadboards and jumper wires make it easy to build and test circuits without soldering, allowing you to experiment with different components and designs.

1. **Breadboards**

   A breadboard is a plastic board with holes arranged in rows and columns for connecting components. Here's how breadboards are typically structured:

   - o **Rows and Columns**: Rows are connected horizontally in groups of five, while columns on the sides (often marked with red and blue lines) are connected vertically as power rails.
   - o **Power Rails**: The power rails run vertically along the sides of the breadboard, and are used to distribute power (VCC and GND) across the board.

- o **Using the Breadboard**: Insert components into the holes, and connect them using jumper wires. The connections will stay secure but can be easily removed or adjusted.

2. **Jumper Wires**

   Jumper wires are flexible cables used to connect components on a breadboard or between a breadboard and the Raspberry Pi's GPIO pins. They come in various colors, helping you keep track of connections. Jumper wires can be male-to-male, female-to-female, or male-to-female, allowing you to connect between different types of pins and sockets.

Quick Exercise: Try setting up a simple breadboard with a resistor and LED. Practice using jumper wires to connect components and get a feel for how they fit into the breadboard.

Building Simple Circuits and Connecting Them to the Raspberry Pi's GPIO Pins

Now that we understand some basic components and how to use a breadboard, let's create a simple circuit and connect it to the Raspberry Pi's GPIO pins.

The Goal: Build a circuit with an LED that lights up when connected to the Raspberry Pi, which will serve as a foundation for controlling components in future chapters.

Understanding GPIO Pins

The Raspberry Pi's GPIO (General Purpose Input/Output) pins allow it to communicate with and control various electronic components. The GPIO pins can be set as input (to read data) or output (to control components like LEDs or motors).

1. **Locate the GPIO Pins**: The GPIO header on the Raspberry Pi has multiple pins, each with a specific function. The standard pins are divided into:
   o **Power Pins**: 3.3V and 5V pins supply power to components.
   o **Ground Pins (GND)**: These pins connect to the ground in your circuits.
   o **GPIO Pins**: The general-purpose input/output pins that can be programmed to send or receive signals.
2. **Setting Up the Circuit**: Let's create a basic circuit to control an LED.

Materials Needed

- 1 LED
- 1 resistor (220Ω or 330Ω, to limit current for the LED)
- Jumper wires
- Breadboard

Step-by-Step Instructions

1. **Insert the LED into the Breadboard**:
   o Place the LED on the breadboard, with its longer leg (anode, +) in one row and its shorter leg (cathode, -) in another row.

2. **Connect a Resistor to the LED**:
   o Insert a 220Ω or 330Ω resistor in series with the LED. Connect one end of the resistor to the same row as the anode of the LED and the other end to a different row.

3. **Connect to Raspberry Pi GPIO**:
   o Use a jumper wire to connect the row with the free end of the resistor to **GPIO Pin 18** on the Raspberry Pi (you can choose another GPIO pin if you prefer, just remember which one).
   o Connect the cathode (shorter leg) of the LED to a ground (GND) pin on the Raspberry Pi using another jumper wire.

Diagram of Connections:

csharp

[GPIO 18] ----> Resistor ----> Anode (long leg) of LED

[Cathode (short leg) of LED] ----> GND

Writing a Python Script to Control the LED

With the circuit in place, let's write a Python script to turn the LED on and off using the Raspberry Pi's GPIO library.

1. Open the Terminal and create a new Python file:

bash

nano led_control.py

2. Write the following code in led_control.py:

python

Copy code

```python
import RPi.GPIO as GPIO
import time

# Set up the GPIO mode and pin
GPIO.setmode(GPIO.BCM)   # Use BCM numbering for GPIO
GPIO.setup(18, GPIO.OUT)  # Set GPIO 18 as an output pin

try:
    # Turn the LED on and off repeatedly
    while True:
        GPIO.output(18, GPIO.HIGH)  # Turn LED on
        print("LED is ON")
        time.sleep(1)  # Wait for 1 second
        GPIO.output(18, GPIO.LOW)  # Turn LED off
        print("LED is OFF")
```

```
time.sleep(1)  # Wait for 1 second
except KeyboardInterrupt:
    # Clean up GPIO settings on exit
    GPIO.cleanup()
    print("Program stopped")
```

Here's a breakdown of the code:

- **GPIO.setmode(GPIO.BCM)**: Sets the GPIO pin numbering scheme.
- **GPIO.setup(18, GPIO.OUT)**: Configures GPIO 18 as an output pin.
- **GPIO.output(18, GPIO.HIGH/LOW)**: Turns the LED on (HIGH) and off (LOW).
- **try-except block**: Allows us to stop the program with Ctrl+C, which calls GPIO.cleanup() to reset the pins.

3. Save the file (**Ctrl + O**) and exit (**Ctrl + X**).
4. Run the program with:

bash

python3 led_control.py

The LED should blink on and off every second, and you'll see messages in the Terminal indicating the LED's status. To stop the program, press **Ctrl + C**.

In this chapter, you learned about key electronic components— resistors, capacitors, and LEDs—and how they function in circuits. You also explored the use of breadboards and jumper wires for building circuits without soldering, making it easier to experiment and test. Finally, you built a simple circuit to control an LED with the Raspberry Pi's GPIO pins and wrote a Python program to make the LED blink.

By mastering these basics, you now have the foundation to connect and control a wide range of components with the Raspberry Pi. In the next chapter, we'll dive deeper into GPIO programming, learning how to interact with other components and start building more complex circuits.

CHAPTER 5: GPIO PROGRAMMING WITH PYTHON

The General Purpose Input/Output (GPIO) pins on the Raspberry Pi allow you to interface with external components such as LEDs, buttons, sensors, and motors. These pins enable you to control devices and read inputs, providing the foundation for adding functionality to your robot. In this chapter, we'll explore how the GPIO pins work, set up the necessary Python libraries, and complete hands-on exercises for controlling LEDs and reading button inputs.

Introduction to the General Purpose Input/Output (GPIO) Pins

The GPIO pins on the Raspberry Pi are versatile interfaces that can send or receive electrical signals, enabling the Pi to interact with electronic components. Here's a breakdown of key concepts:

1. **GPIO Pin Layout and Numbering**
   - The Raspberry Pi has two main pin numbering systems: **BCM** (Broadcom SOC channel numbering) and **BOARD** (physical pin numbering).
   - **BCM** uses the GPIO pin's internal numbering scheme, while **BOARD** refers to the pin's physical position on the header.
   - We'll use BCM numbering for consistency, as it's commonly used in programming examples and libraries.

2. **Types of GPIO Pins**

   o **Power Pins**: Provide power to components. Pins labeled **3.3V** and **5V** supply a constant voltage.

   o **Ground Pins (GND)**: Connect to the ground in your circuits.

   o **GPIO Pins**: Configurable pins used as input or output to control components or read data.

3. **Input vs. Output Modes**

   o **Output Mode**: The GPIO pin sends a signal to control a device, such as turning on an LED or triggering a motor.

   o **Input Mode**: The GPIO pin reads a signal from an external component, such as a button press or a sensor's output.

Important Note: Be cautious with GPIO pins to avoid short circuits or overloading. Always use appropriate resistors and components to ensure safe operation.

Setting Up GPIO Programming Libraries in Python

To control the GPIO pins with Python, we'll use the RPi.GPIO library, which is pre-installed on most versions of Raspberry Pi OS. This library provides simple commands to configure and control the GPIO pins.

1. **Verify RPi.GPIO Installation**

o Most Raspberry Pi OS installations come with RPi.GPIO pre-installed. To verify, open the Terminal and type:

bash
python3 -c "import RPi.GPIO as GPIO"

o If no errors are shown, the library is installed. If it's missing, install it with:

bash
sudo apt update
sudo apt install python3-rpi.gpio

2. **Setting Up GPIO in Python**

o **Import the Library**: Begin by importing RPi.GPIO.

python
import RPi.GPIO as GPIO

o **Choose a Numbering System**: Set the pin numbering mode (BCM or BOARD).

python
Copy code
GPIO.setmode(GPIO.BCM)   #   or
GPIO.setmode(GPIO.BOARD)

o **Configure Pins**: Set the desired pins as input or output.

python

GPIO.setup(pin_number, GPIO.OUT) # Configure as output

GPIO.setup(pin_number, GPIO.IN) # Configure as input

o **Clean Up**: Always clean up the GPIO settings at the end of your program to reset the pins.

python

GPIO.cleanup()

These basics will allow you to configure pins for reading or sending signals, providing the core control needed for your robotics projects.

Hands-on: Controlling LEDs and Reading Button Inputs

Let's practice GPIO programming with two hands-on exercises: controlling an LED (output) and reading a button input. You'll connect these components to the Raspberry Pi and write Python code to control them.

Materials Needed

- 1 LED
- 1 button

- 1 resistor (220Ω for LED)
- 1 resistor (10kΩ for button)
- Breadboard and jumper wires

Exercise 1: Controlling an LED

In this exercise, you'll connect an LED to the Raspberry Pi and control it using Python.

Circuit Setup

1. **Insert the LED into the Breadboard**:
    o   Place the LED on the breadboard, with its longer leg (anode, +) in one row and its shorter leg (cathode, -) in another row.

2. **Add a Resistor to the LED**:
    o   Insert a 220Ω resistor in series with the LED. Connect one end of the resistor to the same row as the LED's anode (+) and the other end to a different row.

3. **Connect to GPIO Pins**:
    o   Use a jumper wire to connect the free end of the resistor to GPIO pin 18 (or another available GPIO pin).
    o   Connect the LED's cathode (shorter leg) to a ground (GND) pin on the Raspberry Pi.

Python Code to Control the LED

1. Open the Terminal and create a new Python file:

bash

Copy code

nano led_blink.py

2. Enter the following code:

```python
import RPi.GPIO as GPIO
import time

# Set up GPIO mode and pin
GPIO.setmode(GPIO.BCM)
GPIO.setup(18, GPIO.OUT)

try:
    # Blink the LED repeatedly
    while True:
        GPIO.output(18, GPIO.HIGH)  # Turn LED on
        print("LED ON")
        time.sleep(1)  # Wait for 1 second
        GPIO.output(18, GPIO.LOW)   # Turn LED off
        print("LED OFF")
        time.sleep(1)  # Wait for 1 second
```

except KeyboardInterrupt:

Clean up GPIO settings on exit

GPIO.cleanup()

print("Program stopped")

3. Save and exit (**Ctrl + O**, **Enter**, then **Ctrl + X**).
4. Run the program:

bash

python3 led_blink.py

The LED should turn on and off every second. You can stop the program with **Ctrl + C**.

Exercise 2: Reading a Button Input

In this exercise, you'll connect a button to the Raspberry Pi and write a Python program to detect when it's pressed.

Circuit Setup

1. **Place the Button on the Breadboard**:
   o Place the button so that each pair of legs is on a separate row. Most buttons connect across the breadboard's middle gap.
2. **Add a 10kΩ Pull-Down Resistor**:
   o Connect one leg of the button to ground (GND) on the Raspberry Pi using a jumper wire.

○ Connect a 10kΩ resistor between the other leg of the button and GND. This is a pull-down resistor, which keeps the input at a low (0) state until the button is pressed.

3. **Connect the Button to GPIO Pin**:

○ Connect the other leg of the button (not connected to the resistor) to **GPIO pin 17** (or another GPIO pin).

Python Code to Detect Button Presses

1. Create a new Python file in Terminal:

bash
nano button_input.py

2. Enter the following code:

python
Copy code
import RPi.GPIO as GPIO
import time

# Set up GPIO mode and pin
GPIO.setmode(GPIO.BCM)

```python
GPIO.setup(17,                                    GPIO.IN,
pull_up_down=GPIO.PUD_DOWN)  # Set pin 17 as input
with pull-down

print("Press the button...")

try:
    # Check for button press
    while True:
        if  GPIO.input(17)  ==  GPIO.HIGH:   # Button is
pressed
            print("Button Pressed!")
            time.sleep(0.5)  # Debounce delay
        else:
            print("Button Released")
            time.sleep(0.5)
except KeyboardInterrupt:
    # Clean up GPIO settings on exit
    GPIO.cleanup()
    print("Program stopped")
```

3. Save and exit (**Ctrl + O, Enter**, then **Ctrl + X**).
4. Run the program:

```bash
bash
python3 button_input.py
```

When you press the button, the program should print "Button Pressed!" and "Button Released" when you let go. To stop the program, press **Ctrl + C**.

Explanation of Pull-Down Resistors and Debouncing

1. **Pull-Down Resistor**: The pull-down resistor (10kΩ in this example) ensures the GPIO pin stays at a low (0) state when the button isn't pressed, preventing floating values and false signals.
2. **Debouncing**: When a button is pressed, it can produce multiple signals as it settles. Adding a small delay (e.g., time.sleep(0.5)) helps filter out these erratic signals, creating a clean, single press detection.

In this chapter, you explored the basics of GPIO programming on the Raspberry Pi. You learned how to set up and control GPIO pins using Python and completed two hands-on exercises: one to control an LED and another to read a button input. These exercises demonstrated how to use GPIO output and input modes, providing you with essential skills for building circuits and controlling devices with the Raspberry Pi.

With this foundational understanding, you're ready to begin adding more complex components and control mechanisms to your robot. In the next chapter, we'll dive into motors and how to control them, enabling your robot to move and respond to commands. Let's keep building!

CHAPTER 6: WORKING WITH MOTORS

Motors are essential components in robotics, as they allow your robot to move and perform tasks. In this chapter, we'll explore the different types of motors commonly used in robotics, how to control them with a Raspberry Pi using motor drivers, and build a basic motor control program in Python. By the end of this chapter, you'll understand how to set up and control DC motors, servo motors, and stepper motors, giving you the ability to bring motion to your robot.

Types of Motors: DC Motors, Servo Motors, and Stepper Motors

Each motor type has unique characteristics suited to different tasks. Let's examine each one:

1. **DC Motors**
   - **Description**: DC (Direct Current) motors are the simplest type of motor, operating when current flows through them. They provide continuous rotational motion and are often used in applications where simple on/off and speed control are required.

- o **Control**: You can control a DC motor's speed by varying the voltage supplied or using Pulse Width Modulation (PWM).
- o **Common Use**: DC motors are typically used in wheels for basic robots, fans, and simple machinery.

2. **Servo Motors**

- o **Description**: Servo motors offer precise control of angular position within a limited range (usually 0 to 180 degrees). Internally, a servo motor has a small DC motor, gears, and a feedback system that allows precise control.
- o **Control**: A servo motor is controlled by a PWM signal, which sets the position of the motor shaft based on the duty cycle.
- o **Common Use**: Servos are used in applications requiring precise angle control, such as controlling robot arms or adjusting a camera's position.

3. **Stepper Motors**

- o **Description**: Stepper motors move in fixed increments or "steps." Unlike DC motors, they rotate in precise steps, allowing you to control both speed and position very accurately.
- o **Control**: Stepper motors require specific step sequences for operation, which are controlled by sending pulses to the motor driver.

o **Common Use**: Stepper motors are ideal for applications requiring precise control, such as 3D printers, CNC machines, and precise robotic arms.

Choosing the Right Motor: The motor type you choose depends on the level of control and precision required. For basic movement, DC motors are usually sufficient, while servo and stepper motors are best suited for applications needing precise angular or step control.

Setting Up Motor Driver Circuits to Control Motors with the Raspberry Pi

Since the Raspberry Pi's GPIO pins cannot supply enough current to drive motors directly, we use motor driver circuits. Motor drivers amplify the low-current signal from the GPIO pins to the level needed by motors. Here's an overview of common motor drivers:

1. **L293D Motor Driver (for DC Motors)**
   o The **L293D** is a popular H-bridge motor driver chip that allows control of two DC motors independently. It supports forward and reverse rotation and provides enough current to drive small to medium-sized DC motors.
   o **Pin Connections**:
     ▪ **IN1/IN2**: Control direction of Motor 1.

- **IN3/IN4**: Control direction of Motor 2.
- **Enable Pins**: Control motor speed through PWM signals.

2. **PWM for Servo Motors**
   o Servo motors are controlled by sending a PWM signal from the Raspberry Pi's GPIO pins directly, without an external driver in many cases. The PWM duty cycle determines the position of the servo arm.

   o **Pin Connection**:
     - Connect the control wire of the servo to a PWM-enabled GPIO pin.
     - Use a separate power source (often 5V) for larger servos to avoid overloading the Raspberry Pi.

3. **ULN2003 Driver Board (for Stepper Motors)**
   o The **ULN2003** is a driver board commonly used for small stepper motors. It contains transistors that amplify the GPIO signals to drive the motor.

   o **Pin Connections**:
     - Connect the stepper motor's four control wires to the driver board, which then connects to the Raspberry Pi's GPIO pins for control.

Hands-on: Building a Basic Motor Control Program in Python

Let's create circuits and code examples to control each motor type.

Exercise 1: Controlling a DC Motor

Materials Needed

- 1 DC motor
- L293D motor driver
- External power source (e.g., 6V battery pack)
- Breadboard and jumper wires

Circuit Setup

1. **Connect the L293D Motor Driver to the Raspberry Pi**:
   o Connect **IN1** to GPIO pin 18 on the Raspberry Pi.
   o Connect **IN2** to GPIO pin 23 on the Raspberry Pi.
   o Connect the **Enable 1** pin (for Motor 1) to GPIO pin 25 to control speed (via PWM).
   o Connect **GND** and **VCC** (5V or external power) to the respective power pins on the motor driver.
2. **Connect the DC Motor**:
   o Attach the two terminals of the DC motor to the **OUT1** and **OUT2** pins on the motor driver.
3. **Power the Circuit**:
   o Connect an external power source to the motor driver's **VCC** and **GND** pins. The Raspberry Pi will control the motor, but an external power source is needed to power it.

Python Code for DC Motor Control

1. Create a new Python file:

```bash
nano dc_motor_control.py
```

2. Write the following code to control the motor's direction and speed:

```python
import RPi.GPIO as GPIO
import time

# Set up GPIO mode and pins
GPIO.setmode(GPIO.BCM)
GPIO.setup(18, GPIO.OUT)  # IN1
GPIO.setup(23, GPIO.OUT)  # IN2
GPIO.setup(25, GPIO.OUT)  # Enable

# Set up PWM on the enable pin
pwm = GPIO.PWM(25, 100)  # 100 Hz
pwm.start(0)  # Start with 0% duty cycle (off)

try:
    # Forward rotation
    GPIO.output(18, GPIO.HIGH)
```

```python
GPIO.output(23, GPIO.LOW)
pwm.ChangeDutyCycle(75)  # 75% speed
time.sleep(2)

# Reverse rotation
GPIO.output(18, GPIO.LOW)
GPIO.output(23, GPIO.HIGH)
pwm.ChangeDutyCycle(50)  # 50% speed
time.sleep(2)

# Stop the motor
pwm.ChangeDutyCycle(0)
except KeyboardInterrupt:
    pass
finally:
    # Clean up GPIO settings
    GPIO.cleanup()
    print("Program stopped")
```

3. Save and run the code. The motor should rotate in one direction, reverse, and then stop.

Exercise 2: Controlling a Servo Motor

Materials Needed

- 1 servo motor

- Breadboard and jumper wires

Circuit Setup

1. **Connect the Servo Motor**:
   - Connect the servo motor's **control wire** (usually white or yellow) to GPIO pin 18 (a PWM-enabled pin) on the Raspberry Pi.
   - Connect the **VCC** and **GND** wires of the servo to a 5V power supply (often provided by the Raspberry Pi, but external power is recommended for larger servos).

Python Code for Servo Control

1. Create a new Python file:

bash

nano servo_control.py

2. Write the following code to control the servo's position:

python

import RPi.GPIO as GPIO

import time

Set up GPIO mode and pin

```python
GPIO.setmode(GPIO.BCM)
GPIO.setup(18, GPIO.OUT)

# Set up PWM
pwm = GPIO.PWM(18, 50)  # 50 Hz (20ms PWM period)
pwm.start(0)  # Start with 0% duty cycle

try:
    # Move to 0 degrees
    pwm.ChangeDutyCycle(2)  # 2% duty cycle
    time.sleep(1)

    # Move to 90 degrees
    pwm.ChangeDutyCycle(7)  # 7% duty cycle
    time.sleep(1)

    # Move to 180 degrees
    pwm.ChangeDutyCycle(12)  # 12% duty cycle
    time.sleep(1)
except KeyboardInterrupt:
    pass
finally:
    pwm.stop()
    GPIO.cleanup()
    print("Program stopped")
```

3. Save and run the code. The servo should move between 0°, 90°, and 180°.

Exercise 3: Controlling a Stepper Motor

Materials Needed

- 1 stepper motor with ULN2003 driver board
- Breadboard and jumper wires

Circuit Setup

1. **Connect the Stepper Motor to ULN2003**:
   - Connect the motor's wires to the ULN2003 driver board.
2. **Connect the Driver Board to the Raspberry Pi**:
   - Connect **IN1** to GPIO 17, **IN2** to GPIO 18, **IN3** to GPIO 27, and **IN4** to GPIO 22 on the Raspberry Pi.

Python Code for Stepper Motor Control

1. Create a new Python file:

bash
nano stepper_control.py

2. Write the following code:

python

```python
Copy code
import RPi.GPIO as GPIO
import time

# Set up GPIO mode and pins
GPIO.setmode(GPIO.BCM)
control_pins = [17, 18, 27, 22]

for pin in control_pins:
    GPIO.setup(pin, GPIO.OUT)
    GPIO.output(pin, 0)

# Define step sequence
seq = [
    [1, 0, 0, 1],
    [1, 0, 0, 0],
    [1, 1, 0, 0],
    [0, 1, 0, 0],
    [0, 1, 1, 0],
    [0, 0, 1, 0],
    [0, 0, 1, 1],
    [0, 0, 0, 1]
]

try:
```

```
for _ in range(512):  # Move 512 steps (one full rotation)
    for step in seq:
        for pin in range(4):
            GPIO.output(control_pins[pin], step[pin])
            time.sleep(0.001)
except KeyboardInterrupt:
    pass
finally:
    GPIO.cleanup()
    print("Program stopped")
```

3. Save and run the code. The stepper motor should rotate one full revolution.

In this chapter, you learned about three common types of motors—DC, servo, and stepper—and how to control them with the Raspberry Pi. You set up motor driver circuits to safely control these motors and wrote Python programs to manage motor direction, speed, and position.

With these skills, you can now make your robot move and perform tasks requiring precision and control. In the next chapter, we'll begin constructing the robot chassis and integrating these motors, laying the groundwork for your first mobile robot!

CHAPTER 7: BUILDING YOUR FIRST SIMPLE ROBOT CHASSIS

In this chapter, we'll focus on the physical structure of your robot: the chassis. The chassis is the foundation of your robot, providing stability and housing for components like motors, batteries, and the Raspberry Pi. We'll start with an overview of common robot chassis designs, assemble a simple wheeled chassis with DC motors, and wire up the motors to test basic movement commands.

Overview of Common Robot Chassis Designs

There are various chassis designs used in robotics, each suited to different types of movement and terrains. Here's an overview of the most common designs:

1. **Two-Wheeled Differential Drive**
    - o **Description**: This is one of the simplest and most popular designs for small robots. It features two powered wheels on either side, with each wheel

driven by a separate motor. A caster or omni-directional wheel supports the rear, allowing the robot to balance.

- o **Pros**: Simple to control; can pivot in place, making it highly maneuverable.
- o **Cons**: Limited stability and traction on uneven surfaces.
- o **Common Uses**: Educational robots, indoor robots, small hobby robots.

2. **Four-Wheeled Drive**

- o **Description**: A chassis with four powered wheels, each driven by a separate motor or paired motors. It provides more stability and traction than a two-wheeled design.
- o **Pros**: Good stability and can handle uneven terrain better than a two-wheeled robot.
- o **Cons**: More complex control and wiring, increased power consumption.
- o **Common Uses**: Outdoor robots, larger autonomous robots, robots requiring more stability.

3. **Tracked or Tank-Style**

- o **Description**: This design uses continuous tracks instead of wheels, similar to a tank. The tracks provide excellent traction and stability on a variety of surfaces.

- o **Pros**: High stability and traction; suitable for rough and uneven terrain.
- o **Cons**: Complex mechanics and higher power requirements; slower speeds compared to wheeled robots.
- o **Common Uses**: Robots designed for outdoor exploration or rough terrains, rescue robots.

Choosing a Chassis Design: For our project, we'll build a simple two-wheeled differential drive robot. This design is easy to assemble and control, making it ideal for beginners. You can later expand or upgrade your robot with a four-wheel or tracked chassis as you gain experience.

Assembling a Simple Wheeled Chassis with DC Motors

Let's assemble a basic two-wheeled robot chassis that uses DC motors for propulsion. Here's what you'll need for the assembly:

Materials Needed

- 1 two-wheeled robot chassis kit (including two DC motors, two wheels, and a caster wheel)
- Motor mounts (if not included in your chassis kit)
- Screws and nuts (often included with the kit)
- Screwdriver
- Battery holder (for powering motors)

Step-by-Step Assembly Instructions

1. **Attach the DC Motors to the Chassis**
   - Secure the DC motors to the chassis using motor mounts and screws. Place each motor on opposite sides of the chassis so that each motor drives one wheel.
   - Ensure that the motors are securely attached and align with the sides of the chassis to keep the wheels stable.

2. **Attach the Wheels to the Motors**
   - Push the wheels onto the output shafts of each DC motor until they fit snugly.
   - Verify that the wheels spin freely when the motor shafts are rotated.

3. **Install the Caster Wheel**
   - Attach the caster wheel (the small, omni-directional support wheel) to the rear of the chassis. This wheel stabilizes the robot and allows it to pivot.
   - Ensure that the caster wheel can move smoothly in all directions.

4. **Add a Battery Holder**
   - Place the battery holder on the chassis (often there is a slot or mount specifically for the batteries).
   - Secure it in place with screws or zip ties if necessary.

5. **Mount the Raspberry Pi (Optional)**

   o If your chassis has space, you can mount the Raspberry Pi to the chassis using mounting holes and screws. However, for initial testing, you may leave the Raspberry Pi nearby on a stable surface.

Your basic robot chassis should now be assembled! Next, we'll wire up the motors and test basic movement commands to ensure the motors and chassis function as expected.

Wiring Up the Motors and Testing Basic Movement Commands

To control the DC motors, we'll use the L293D motor driver (or an L298N motor driver if preferred). The motor driver allows us to control each motor independently, enabling the robot to move forward, backward, and turn.

Circuit Setup

1. **Connect the L293D Motor Driver to the Raspberry Pi**:
   o Connect **IN1** to GPIO pin 18 on the Raspberry Pi.
   o Connect **IN2** to GPIO pin 23 on the Raspberry Pi.
   o Connect **IN3** to GPIO pin 24 on the Raspberry Pi.
   o Connect **IN4** to GPIO pin 25 on the Raspberry Pi.
   o Connect the **Enable 1** pin (for Motor 1) to GPIO pin 17, and **Enable 2** (for Motor 2) to GPIO pin 27. These will control the speed of each motor through PWM.

2. **Connect the Motors to the Motor Driver**:
   - Attach one motor to the **OUT1** and **OUT2** terminals on the motor driver.
   - Attach the second motor to the **OUT3** and **OUT4** terminals.

3. **Power the Circuit**:
   - Connect an external power source (battery pack) to the motor driver's **VCC** and **GND** pins to power the motors.
   - Connect the Raspberry Pi's **GND** to the motor driver's **GND** to share a common ground.

Python Code to Test Basic Movement Commands

Now that the hardware is set up, let's write a Python program to control the motors and test basic movement commands (forward, backward, turn left, turn right).

1. Open the Terminal and create a new Python file:

   bash
   nano motor_test.py

2. Write the following code to control the motors:

   python
   import RPi.GPIO as GPIO
   import time

```python
# Set up GPIO mode
GPIO.setmode(GPIO.BCM)

# Motor pins
IN1 = 18
IN2 = 23
IN3 = 24
IN4 = 25
ENA = 17
ENB = 27

# Set up motor pins
GPIO.setup(IN1, GPIO.OUT)
GPIO.setup(IN2, GPIO.OUT)
GPIO.setup(IN3, GPIO.OUT)
GPIO.setup(IN4, GPIO.OUT)
GPIO.setup(ENA, GPIO.OUT)
GPIO.setup(ENB, GPIO.OUT)

# Set up PWM on Enable pins
pwmA = GPIO.PWM(ENA, 100)
pwmB = GPIO.PWM(ENB, 100)
pwmA.start(50)  # 50% speed
pwmB.start(50)  # 50% speed
```

```python
# Functions to control the motors
def forward():
    GPIO.output(IN1, GPIO.HIGH)
    GPIO.output(IN2, GPIO.LOW)
    GPIO.output(IN3, GPIO.HIGH)
    GPIO.output(IN4, GPIO.LOW)

def backward():
    GPIO.output(IN1, GPIO.LOW)
    GPIO.output(IN2, GPIO.HIGH)
    GPIO.output(IN3, GPIO.LOW)
    GPIO.output(IN4, GPIO.HIGH)

def turn_left():
    GPIO.output(IN1, GPIO.LOW)
    GPIO.output(IN2, GPIO.HIGH)
    GPIO.output(IN3, GPIO.HIGH)
    GPIO.output(IN4, GPIO.LOW)

def turn_right():
    GPIO.output(IN1, GPIO.HIGH)
    GPIO.output(IN2, GPIO.LOW)
    GPIO.output(IN3, GPIO.LOW)
    GPIO.output(IN4, GPIO.HIGH)
```

```python
def stop():
    GPIO.output(IN1, GPIO.LOW)
    GPIO.output(IN2, GPIO.LOW)
    GPIO.output(IN3, GPIO.LOW)
    GPIO.output(IN4, GPIO.LOW)

# Test movement
try:
    print("Moving forward")
    forward()
    time.sleep(2)

    print("Moving backward")
    backward()
    time.sleep(2)

    print("Turning left")
    turn_left()
    time.sleep(2)

    print("Turning right")
    turn_right()
    time.sleep(2)
```

```
print("Stopping")
stop()
except KeyboardInterrupt:
    pass
finally:
    GPIO.cleanup()
    print("Program stopped")
```

3. Save and exit the file (**Ctrl + O, Enter**, then **Ctrl + X**).
4. Run the code to test the movement commands:

```bash
python3 motor_test.py
```

Expected Results: The robot should perform the following movements:

- Move forward for 2 seconds
- Move backward for 2 seconds
- Turn left for 2 seconds
- Turn right for 2 seconds
- Stop

You can adjust the motor speeds by changing the duty cycle (50% in this example) of the pwmA and pwmB PWM signals.

In this chapter, you assembled a basic two-wheeled robot chassis, wired up the DC motors using an L293D motor driver, and wrote a

Python program to test basic movement commands. This setup forms the foundation of your robot, enabling it to perform basic maneuvers. You now have a mobile platform to which you can add sensors, controls, and more advanced functionalities.

In the next chapter, we'll dive into powering your robot and managing power sources effectively. This will ensure your robot runs reliably and safely as we add more components and functionality.

Chapter 8: Powering Your Robot

Powering your robot effectively is essential for smooth and reliable operation. This chapter covers the basics of powering the Raspberry Pi, choosing the right power source for your robot, and wiring it up correctly. We'll also discuss power management and safety tips to prevent issues like overheating, power surges, and accidental damage.

Powering the Raspberry Pi: Batteries vs. External Power Sources

The Raspberry Pi needs a stable 5V power source to function correctly. Let's explore the most common options for powering both the Raspberry Pi and other components of your robot.

1. **Using Batteries**

     o **Battery Packs**: A portable battery pack or rechargeable battery pack is a popular choice, especially if you want a fully mobile robot. Many packs provide 5V via USB, making them compatible with the Raspberry Pi's power input.

- o **Battery Types**: Common types include **lithium-ion (Li-Ion)**, **lithium-polymer (LiPo)**, and **AA battery packs**. Each has its pros and cons:
    - **Li-Ion** and **LiPo** batteries provide high capacity and low weight but require careful handling and proper chargers.
    - **AA Battery Packs** (6x AA batteries can provide ~9V) can work with a voltage regulator to step down to 5V for the Raspberry Pi.

2. **External Power Sources**
    - o **Wall Adapters**: If your robot doesn't need to be mobile (e.g., during testing), a wall adapter is ideal. A 5V/3A power supply is recommended for the Raspberry Pi 4, as it can handle the Pi's power needs along with some connected components.
    - o **USB Power Banks**: Portable USB power banks are compatible with the Pi's micro-USB or USB-C power port. Ensure the power bank provides at least 2.5A for Raspberry Pi models requiring more current.

3. **Power Requirements for Motors and Sensors**
    - o Motors often require more power than the Raspberry Pi itself, so you may need a separate battery pack dedicated to motors.

- o It's common to use a higher-voltage power source (e.g., 6V or 9V) for the motors and a 5V power source for the Raspberry Pi. A **common ground** between these sources is necessary for them to communicate effectively.

Choosing and Wiring a Power Source for Your Robot

Choosing the right power source depends on factors like mobility, battery life, and safety. Here are steps and guidelines for selecting and wiring a power source for your robot.

Step 1: Selecting the Right Battery Type

1. **Determine Power Requirements**
   - o Calculate the current requirements of each component (Raspberry Pi, motors, sensors).
   - o The Raspberry Pi 4 requires around **5V/3A** for stable operation, especially with accessories like cameras or sensors.
   - o Motors may require 6V-12V depending on the type and can draw considerable current (often 1A or more).

2. **Battery Capacity (mAh)**

- o Choose a battery with enough capacity (measured in milliamp-hours, mAh) to support the desired runtime.
- o For example, a 5000mAh battery pack providing 5V to the Raspberry Pi alone could last for around **5000mAh / 3000mA = ~1.6 hours**.

3. **Separate Batteries for Motors and Raspberry Pi (Recommended)**
   - o To avoid power fluctuations and potential interference, it's best to use separate batteries: one for the Raspberry Pi (5V) and one for the motors (e.g., 6V or 9V).
   - o Use a **voltage regulator** if necessary to step down the voltage from a higher battery pack to 5V.

Step 2: Wiring the Power Sources

1. **Powering the Raspberry Pi**
   - o If you're using a USB power bank or battery pack, connect it to the Pi's USB-C or micro-USB power input.
   - o If using a custom battery solution (e.g., LiPo or AA batteries), use a **5V UBEC (Universal Battery Elimination Circuit)** or a **5V voltage regulator** to step down to a stable 5V and wire it to the GPIO 5V pin.

2. **Powering the Motors**

   o Connect a separate battery pack (e.g., 6V or 9V) to the motor driver's **VCC** and **GND** pins. This power source should be appropriate for your motor specifications.

   o Ensure you connect the motor battery's ground to the Raspberry Pi's ground if you want to control the motor with the Pi.

3. **Connecting Grounds**

   o Connect the ground (GND) from the Raspberry Pi to the ground of the motor driver and all other components. A common ground ensures consistent electrical reference across all parts of the robot.

Power Management and Safety Tips

1. **Use Voltage Regulators for Stability**

   o If you're using a battery that outputs more than 5V (e.g., 9V or 12V), add a **5V regulator** to step down the voltage for the Raspberry Pi.

   o For motors, make sure your power source matches the motor's voltage specifications. If not, use a **voltage regulator**.

2. **Avoid Overloading the Raspberry Pi's GPIO**

- o Do not power motors directly from the GPIO pins, as they cannot supply enough current and may damage the Raspberry Pi.
- o Always use a motor driver (like L293D or L298N) or a separate battery for motors.

3. **Protect Against Overheating**

- o Motors and other high-power components can generate heat. Place the Raspberry Pi and sensitive electronics away from heat sources, and consider adding heat sinks to the Raspberry Pi if it runs hot.
- o For high-power robots, ensure good ventilation or use a fan to cool the Pi.

4. **Use Fuses for Additional Protection**

- o Adding a fuse between your battery and the power input can prevent damage from electrical faults or short circuits.
- o Choose a fuse rated slightly above your expected current draw (e.g., a 4A fuse for a setup drawing 3A).

5. **Power On/Off Switch**

- o Adding an on/off switch to your battery pack can prevent accidental power-ups and make it easy to turn off the robot when not in use.

6. **Battery Safety**

o If using LiPo or Li-Ion batteries, follow proper safety guidelines, including using compatible chargers and not over-discharging them.

o Avoid overloading AA battery packs, as alkaline AA batteries are not designed for high current draw and may leak or overheat.

Example: Wiring a Power Setup for Your Robot

Let's look at a practical example of wiring power for a robot with separate sources for the Raspberry Pi and motors.

Materials Needed

- 1 USB power bank (or 5V battery pack) for the Raspberry Pi
- 1 AA battery pack (or 6V-9V battery) for the motors
- 1 L293D motor driver (or L298N)
- Voltage regulator (optional, if using a higher voltage battery)

Wiring Diagram:

1. **Powering the Raspberry Pi**:
   o Connect the USB power bank to the Pi's micro-USB or USB-C power port.

2. **Powering the Motors**:

- o Connect the AA battery pack's positive lead (+) to the **VCC** input on the motor driver.
- o Connect the battery pack's negative lead (−) to the motor driver's **GND**.

3. **Connecting Grounds**:
   - o Connect the ground from the battery pack to the Raspberry Pi's ground.
   - o Connect the motor driver's ground to the Raspberry Pi's ground as well. This common ground is crucial for stable communication.

Testing the Power Setup

1. **Check Voltage with a Multimeter**
   - o Before connecting the Raspberry Pi and motors, use a multimeter to confirm the voltage from each battery source.
   - o For the Raspberry Pi's power source, ensure it's outputting a stable 5V. For the motor power source, confirm it's within the motor's specified range (e.g., 6V-9V).

2. **Power On the Raspberry Pi and Motors**
   - o With everything connected, power on the Raspberry Pi first, and then power the motor driver.
   - o Run a simple motor test program to confirm that the motors respond to commands from the Raspberry Pi.

3. **Observe Operation**

   o Watch for signs of instability, like overheating, unexpected shutdowns, or flickering LED indicators. These may indicate power issues or loose connections.

   o If issues arise, turn off the power, check connections, and ensure components are correctly rated for the current being supplied.

In this chapter, we discussed the essentials of powering your robot, including options for powering the Raspberry Pi with batteries or external sources, selecting the right power source for both the Pi and motors, and wiring them together safely. You also learned essential tips for managing power safely, including using voltage regulators, connecting grounds, and avoiding GPIO overloads.

With a stable power setup, your robot is now equipped for more complex tasks and extended operation. In the next chapter, we'll start adding sensors to your robot, enabling it to perceive and interact with its environment. This will be a big step forward in making your robot autonomous and responsive!

CHAPTER 9: ADDING BASIC SENSORS

Sensors are the "senses" of a robot, allowing it to interact with and respond to its environment. In this chapter, we'll introduce common sensors used in robotics, explain how they communicate with the Raspberry Pi, and complete a hands-on exercise to measure distance using an ultrasonic sensor. By the end, you'll understand how to integrate basic sensors into your robot, laying the foundation for autonomous behavior.

Introduction to Sensors in Robotics

Sensors provide data about the environment, enabling a robot to make decisions. Let's explore some commonly used sensors in robotics:

1. **Ultrasonic Sensors**
   - o **Purpose**: Used to measure the distance between the robot and objects in its path by emitting sound waves and calculating the time it takes for the echo to return.
   - o **Common Use**: Obstacle detection and navigation in mobile robots.
   - o **Example**: HC-SR04 ultrasonic sensor.

2. **Infrared (IR) Sensors**
   - o **Purpose**: IR sensors emit infrared light and detect reflections from objects. They can measure proximity or detect black/white surfaces (often used in line-following robots).
   - o **Common Use**: Line following, proximity detection, object tracking.
   - o **Example**: IR proximity sensor or IR line-tracking sensor.

3. **Temperature Sensors**
   - o **Purpose**: Measure ambient or object temperature. Common in robots that monitor environmental conditions or need to adapt to temperature changes.

- o **Common Use**: Environmental monitoring, industrial robots, climate control.
- o **Example**: DHT11 or DHT22 temperature and humidity sensor.

Choosing the Right Sensor: The sensor you choose depends on your robot's purpose. For this chapter, we'll focus on using an **ultrasonic sensor** to enable basic distance measurement and obstacle detection, which is essential for autonomous navigation.

How Sensors Connect to and Communicate with the Raspberry Pi

Sensors connect to the Raspberry Pi through its GPIO pins, typically using one of these communication methods:

1. **Digital (Binary) Communication**
   - o Some sensors output a digital signal (high or low) to represent data, like IR sensors detecting line edges.
   - o These sensors are straightforward to interface, as they only require a digital input pin.

2. **Analog Communication**
   - o Analog sensors output a variable voltage proportional to the measurement (e.g., light or temperature level).

o The Raspberry Pi lacks analog input pins, so you'll need an **analog-to-digital converter (ADC)** to read analog data.

3. **I2C and SPI Protocols**

o Some sensors communicate via I2C or SPI, which are serial communication protocols. The Raspberry Pi supports both, allowing you to connect multiple sensors with a shared bus for data transfer.

4. **Pulse Width Modulation (PWM) for Ultrasonic Sensors**

o Ultrasonic sensors typically use pulse width modulation (PWM) to send and receive signals. The sensor emits an ultrasonic pulse, then listens for the echo. The time delay between sending and receiving the pulse indicates the distance.

Hands-on: Reading Data from an Ultrasonic Sensor to Measure Distance

Let's dive into a hands-on exercise to connect an ultrasonic sensor to the Raspberry Pi and read distance measurements.

Materials Needed

- 1 HC-SR04 ultrasonic sensor
- Breadboard and jumper wires

Understanding the HC-SR04 Ultrasonic Sensor

The HC-SR04 is a widely used ultrasonic sensor in robotics, with four pins:

1. **VCC**: Power supply (5V)
2. **GND**: Ground
3. **TRIG**: Trigger pin to start the measurement
4. **ECHO**: Echo pin to receive the return signal

How It Works:

1. The Raspberry Pi sends a signal to the **TRIG** pin to initiate a pulse.
2. The sensor sends out an ultrasonic wave and waits for it to reflect back.
3. When the wave returns, the sensor pulls the **ECHO** pin high.
4. The Raspberry Pi measures the time between sending the pulse and receiving the echo to calculate the distance based on the speed of sound.

Distance Calculation Formula:

Distance=Time (in seconds)×Speed of Sound (343 m/s)2\text{Dist ance} = \frac{\text{Time (in seconds)} \times \text{Speed of

Sound (343

m/s)}}{2}Distance=2Time (in seconds)×Speed of Sound (343 m/s)

Wiring the Ultrasonic Sensor to the Raspberry Pi

1. **Power the Sensor**
   - Connect the **VCC** pin on the HC-SR04 to the Raspberry Pi's **5V** pin.
   - Connect the **GND** pin on the HC-SR04 to the Raspberry Pi's **GND**.

2. **Connect the TRIG and ECHO Pins**
   - Connect the **TRIG** pin on the HC-SR04 to **GPIO 23** on the Raspberry Pi.
   - Connect the **ECHO** pin on the HC-SR04 to **GPIO 24** on the Raspberry Pi.

Note: The **ECHO** pin outputs a 5V signal, which the Raspberry Pi's GPIO pins are not designed to handle directly. Use a **voltage divider** (two resistors, e.g., 1kΩ and 2kΩ) on the ECHO line to step down the voltage to ~3.3V.

Voltage Divider Setup:

- Connect a 2kΩ resistor between the **ECHO** pin and **GPIO 24**.

- Connect a 1kΩ resistor between **GPIO 24** and **GND**.

Writing a Python Program to Read Distance

Let's create a Python script to control the ultrasonic sensor and calculate the distance.

1. Open the Terminal and create a new Python file:

   bash

   nano distance_measurement.py

2. Write the following code:

   python
   Copy code

```python
import RPi.GPIO as GPIO
import time

# Set up GPIO mode
GPIO.setmode(GPIO.BCM)

# Define GPIO pins
TRIG = 23
ECHO = 24
```

```python
# Set up the GPIO pins
GPIO.setup(TRIG, GPIO.OUT)
GPIO.setup(ECHO, GPIO.IN)

def measure_distance():
    # Trigger a pulse
    GPIO.output(TRIG, True)
    time.sleep(0.00001)  # Send a 10µs pulse
    GPIO.output(TRIG, False)

    # Wait for the echo to start
    while GPIO.input(ECHO) == 0:
        start_time = time.time()

    # Wait for the echo to end
    while GPIO.input(ECHO) == 1:
        end_time = time.time()

    # Calculate time difference
    duration = end_time - start_time

    # Calculate distance in cm
    distance = (duration * 34300) / 2  # Speed of sound is 34300 cm/s
    return distance
```

```
try:
    while True:
        dist = measure_distance()
        print(f"Distance: {dist:.2f} cm")
        time.sleep(1)  # Wait before the next measurement
except KeyboardInterrupt:
    print("Measurement stopped by user")
finally:
    GPIO.cleanup()
```

3. Save and exit the file (**Ctrl + O, Enter**, then **Ctrl + X**).

Running the Program

Run the program to see distance measurements:

bash

python3 distance_measurement.py

Expected Output: The terminal should display the distance in centimeters, updating every second. You can test by moving an object closer to or farther from the sensor to see how the distance changes.

Explanation of the Code:

- **Triggering the Pulse**: A 10-microsecond pulse is sent to the TRIG pin to start the measurement.
- **Timing the Echo**: The time difference between sending and receiving the pulse (from the ECHO pin) is measured to calculate the distance.
- **Distance Calculation**: The duration is multiplied by the speed of sound (34300 cm/s) and divided by 2 to obtain the distance to the object.

Using the Ultrasonic Sensor in Robotics Applications

Now that you can measure distance, you can apply this functionality to robotic tasks. Here are some potential applications:

1. **Obstacle Avoidance**: Mount the sensor on the front of your robot, continuously measuring distance. Program the robot to stop or change direction if an object is detected within a certain range.
2. **Wall Following**: Position the sensor on the side of the robot and use distance measurements to keep the robot parallel to a wall.
3. **Edge Detection**: If mounted at an angle, the sensor can detect table edges or gaps to prevent the robot from falling.

In this chapter, you learned about essential sensors used in robotics and how to connect them to the Raspberry Pi. We focused on the HC-SR04 ultrasonic sensor, wiring it up to the Raspberry Pi and writing a Python program to measure distance based on the speed of sound. By adding sensors, you've equipped your robot to perceive its surroundings, a critical capability for building autonomous behavior.

In the next chapter, we'll explore how to control your robot remotely using a smartphone or other wireless devices, allowing you to steer or command the robot without physical interaction. This will add flexibility and control as you continue building more advanced capabilities.

CHAPTER 10: CONTROLLING YOUR ROBOT WITH A REMOTE OR SMARTPHONE

Being able to control your robot remotely provides greater flexibility and allows you to operate it from a distance. In this chapter, we'll explore different methods for remote control, set up Bluetooth on the Raspberry Pi, and build a simple Bluetooth remote control system using a smartphone. By the end, you'll be able to control your robot's movement with your smartphone, giving you a foundational skill for more advanced remote or autonomous operation.

Overview of Remote Control Options

There are multiple ways to control a robot remotely. Each method has its advantages and best-use cases depending on the range, responsiveness, and flexibility required.

1. **Wi-Fi (Using SSH or Web-based Control)**
   o **Description**: With Wi-Fi, you can control the Raspberry Pi over a local network, allowing more flexibility and range within the network's coverage.
   o **Pros**: Good range and can transmit larger amounts of data. Allows for web-based control interfaces and real-time video streaming.
   o **Cons**: Requires a Wi-Fi connection, which may not be suitable for outdoor or isolated areas without network coverage.
   o **Use Case**: Ideal for controlling a robot from a laptop or smartphone via a web-based interface.

2. **Bluetooth**
   o **Description**: Bluetooth provides a wireless, short-range communication method that's easy to set up and supported by most smartphones.

- o **Pros**: Simple, reliable for close-range control, and doesn't require an internet connection.
- o **Cons**: Limited range (typically around 10 meters) and slower data transfer compared to Wi-Fi.
- o **Use Case**: Ideal for close-range applications where a smartphone or Bluetooth remote control can be used to operate the robot.

3. **Radio Frequency (RF) Modules**
   - o **Description**: RF modules (like NRF24L01 or 433MHz transmitters) enable long-range communication for outdoor environments without Wi-Fi or Bluetooth coverage.
   - o **Pros**: Good range (up to several hundred meters) and highly reliable.
   - o **Cons**: More complex setup and usually limited to sending simple commands.
   - o **Use Case**: Suitable for long-range outdoor robots or drones.

For this chapter, we'll focus on **Bluetooth** since it is simple, widely supported by smartphones, and easy to set up with the Raspberry Pi.

Setting Up Bluetooth on the Raspberry Pi

Before creating a Bluetooth-controlled robot, let's configure the Raspberry Pi's Bluetooth settings.

1. **Enable Bluetooth on the Raspberry Pi**

   o Ensure Bluetooth is enabled on the Raspberry Pi. Most Raspberry Pi models from the Pi 3 and later have built-in Bluetooth. For older models, you may need a Bluetooth USB dongle.

   o Open a Terminal on the Raspberry Pi and check for Bluetooth support:

   bash

   bluetoothctl

   o If Bluetooth is enabled, you should see a prompt like Agent registered.

2. **Pairing with Your Smartphone**

   o Open the **Bluetooth settings** on your smartphone and enable Bluetooth.

   o In the Raspberry Pi Terminal, run the following commands:

   bash

   bluetoothctl

   This will open the Bluetooth control interface.

   o Turn on the Bluetooth controller:

   bash

   power on

o   Make the Raspberry Pi discoverable:

bash

discoverable on

o   Scan for devices:

bash

scan on

o   You should see your smartphone's name in the list of devices. Copy the MAC address (a string like XX:XX:XX:XX:XX:XX).

o   Pair with your smartphone:

bash

pair XX:XX:XX:XX:XX:XX

o   You may need to confirm the pairing code on your phone.

3. **Connecting to the Device**

o   After pairing, connect to your smartphone:

bash

connect XX:XX:XX:XX:XX:XX

    o   Once connected, you can now use the smartphone to communicate with the Raspberry Pi over Bluetooth.

Hands-on: Building a Simple Bluetooth Remote Control for Your Robot Using a Smartphone

Now, let's create a simple Bluetooth-controlled interface that allows you to send commands from your smartphone to control the robot's movement.

Materials Needed

- Raspberry Pi with Bluetooth enabled
- Bluetooth-capable smartphone
- A terminal app (like Bluetooth Terminal or Serial Bluetooth Terminal) on your smartphone

Step 1: Writing the Python Program on the Raspberry Pi

1. Create a new Python file on the Raspberry Pi:

bash

nano bluetooth_control.py

2. Write the following code to set up a Bluetooth server that listens for commands and controls the robot's movement accordingly:

```python
import RPi.GPIO as GPIO
import time
import bluetooth

# Set up GPIO mode
GPIO.setmode(GPIO.BCM)

# Motor pins
IN1 = 18
IN2 = 23
IN3 = 24
IN4 = 25
ENA = 17
ENB = 27

# Set up motor pins
GPIO.setup(IN1, GPIO.OUT)
GPIO.setup(IN2, GPIO.OUT)
GPIO.setup(IN3, GPIO.OUT)
GPIO.setup(IN4, GPIO.OUT)
GPIO.setup(ENA, GPIO.OUT)
```

```python
GPIO.setup(ENB, GPIO.OUT)

# Set up PWM on Enable pins
pwmA = GPIO.PWM(ENA, 100)
pwmB = GPIO.PWM(ENB, 100)
pwmA.start(50)  # Start at 50% speed
pwmB.start(50)  # Start at 50% speed

# Define functions for robot movement
def move_forward():
    GPIO.output(IN1, GPIO.HIGH)
    GPIO.output(IN2, GPIO.LOW)
    GPIO.output(IN3, GPIO.HIGH)
    GPIO.output(IN4, GPIO.LOW)

def move_backward():
    GPIO.output(IN1, GPIO.LOW)
    GPIO.output(IN2, GPIO.HIGH)
    GPIO.output(IN3, GPIO.LOW)
    GPIO.output(IN4, GPIO.HIGH)

def turn_left():
    GPIO.output(IN1, GPIO.LOW)
    GPIO.output(IN2, GPIO.HIGH)
    GPIO.output(IN3, GPIO.HIGH)
```

```python
    GPIO.output(IN4, GPIO.LOW)

def turn_right():
    GPIO.output(IN1, GPIO.HIGH)
    GPIO.output(IN2, GPIO.LOW)
    GPIO.output(IN3, GPIO.LOW)
    GPIO.output(IN4, GPIO.HIGH)

def stop():
    GPIO.output(IN1, GPIO.LOW)
    GPIO.output(IN2, GPIO.LOW)
    GPIO.output(IN3, GPIO.LOW)
    GPIO.output(IN4, GPIO.LOW)

# Set up Bluetooth server
server_socket = bluetooth.BluetoothSocket(bluetooth.RFCOMM)
port = 1
server_socket.bind(("", port))
server_socket.listen(1)

print("Waiting for Bluetooth connection...")
client_socket, address = server_socket.accept()
print(f"Connected to {address}")
```

```python
try:
    while True:
        # Receive data from the smartphone
        data = client_socket.recv(1024).decode("utf-8").strip()
        print(f"Received: {data}")

        # Execute command based on received data
        if data == "forward":
            move_forward()
        elif data == "backward":
            move_backward()
        elif data == "left":
            turn_left()
        elif data == "right":
            turn_right()
        elif data == "stop":
            stop()
        else:
            print("Unknown command")
except KeyboardInterrupt:
    print("Program interrupted")
finally:
    stop()
    GPIO.cleanup()
    client_socket.close()
```

```
server_socket.close()
print("Connection closed")
```

3. Save and exit the file (**Ctrl + O, Enter**, then **Ctrl + X**).

Step 2: Testing the Program

1. Run the Python program on the Raspberry Pi:

```
bash
python3 bluetooth_control.py
```

2. On your smartphone, open a Bluetooth terminal app (such as **Serial Bluetooth Terminal** on Android).

3. Connect to the Raspberry Pi via Bluetooth in the app and send commands to control the robot:
   - **forward** – Move the robot forward
   - **backward** – Move the robot backward
   - **left** – Turn the robot left
   - **right** – Turn the robot right
   - **stop** – Stop the robot

Expected Behavior: The robot should respond to each command sent from the smartphone, moving in the specified direction or stopping based on the input.

Explanation of the Code

- **Bluetooth Setup**: The program sets up a Bluetooth server on the Raspberry Pi, waiting for a connection from the smartphone. Once connected, it continuously listens for commands.

- **Command Interpretation**: Commands received over Bluetooth are processed in the while loop. Depending on the command (forward, backward, left, right, or stop), the appropriate function is called to control the motors.

- **Robot Movement**: Each movement function uses GPIO output to control the motor driver, adjusting the robot's movement as specified.

Expanding on Bluetooth Control

Once you're comfortable with basic Bluetooth control, consider expanding the code to:

- Adjust speed based on additional commands (e.g., **speed up** or **slow down**).
- Add other control features like **spin** or **reverse turn**.
- Implement additional sensors to send data back to the smartphone for feedback, creating an interactive remote-control experience.

In this chapter, we explored the various options for remotely controlling your robot, including Wi-Fi, Bluetooth, and RF modules. We focused on Bluetooth for its simplicity and ease of integration with smartphones, setting up Bluetooth on the Raspberry Pi and using it to receive control commands from a smartphone. By creating a Bluetooth server, you successfully built a remote control system that lets you steer the robot with simple text commands.

In the next chapter, we'll add more intelligence to the robot by using programming techniques to make it respond to its environment, such as navigating obstacles or following pre-programmed paths. With Bluetooth control in place, you have a flexible way to interact with your robot as we expand its capabilities.

CHAPTER 11: PROGRAMMING BASIC MOVEMENTS AND CONTROL LOOPS

In this chapter, we'll focus on programming fundamental movement patterns for your robot and introduce control loops, which allow the robot to perform continuous movement and respond to commands dynamically. You'll learn to program basic movements like forward, backward, and turning, then use control loops to make your robot follow movement instructions. By the end, you'll be able to control your robot's motion programmatically, laying the groundwork for more advanced autonomous behavior.

Basic Robot Movement Patterns: Forward, Backward, Turning

Basic movement patterns are essential for any mobile robot. Let's break down these fundamental commands, which are particularly useful when navigating environments or following a path.

1. **Moving Forward and Backward**
   - o **Forward**: For a two-wheeled differential drive robot, moving forward involves both motors turning in the same direction (clockwise or counterclockwise).
   - o **Backward**: Similar to moving forward, but both motors turn in the opposite direction.
2. **Turning Left and Right**

o **Left Turn**: To turn left, the right motor continues moving forward while the left motor stops or moves backward.

o **Right Turn**: Similarly, to turn right, the left motor continues moving forward while the right motor stops or moves backward.

3. **Rotating in Place**

o **In-Place Left Turn**: Rotate the robot by making the left motor turn backward and the right motor turn forward.

o **In-Place Right Turn**: Rotate in the opposite direction by making the left motor turn forward and the right motor turn backward.

Each of these movements can be programmed with GPIO outputs on the Raspberry Pi. By controlling the signals sent to each motor, you can implement any of these movement patterns.

Introduction to Control Loops and Programming Continuous Movement

Control loops allow the robot to perform continuous movement until certain conditions are met, such as reaching a target distance, stopping upon an obstacle, or changing direction. Let's look at two main types of control loops:

1. **While Loops**: A while loop repeatedly executes a block of code as long as a specified condition is true.
   - o **Example**: Moving the robot forward until it reaches a certain distance.
2. **For Loops**: A for loop executes a block of code a specific number of times. This is useful for time-bound or step-bound actions.
   - o **Example**: Moving forward for a specific number of steps or a certain duration.

Control loops are crucial for making the robot execute continuous commands without requiring individual inputs for each action.

Example of a Basic Control Loop: Suppose we want the robot to move forward for a set amount of time or until it receives a stop command. A while loop can keep the robot moving until a certain condition (like user input or a timer) is met.

Hands-on: Programming the Robot to Follow Simple Movement Commands

Now let's put these concepts together and create a Python program that makes the robot follow basic movement commands using control loops.

Materials Needed

- Raspberry Pi with GPIO pins connected to motor driver (L293D or L298N)
- Robot with two DC motors

Step 1: Setting Up the Python Program

1. Open the Terminal on your Raspberry Pi and create a new Python file:

   bash
   nano movement_control.py

2. Write the following code to set up movement functions and control loops:

   python
   import RPi.GPIO as GPIO
   import time

   # Set up GPIO mode
   GPIO.setmode(GPIO.BCM)

   # Motor pins
   IN1 = 18
   IN2 = 23
   IN3 = 24
   IN4 = 25

```python
ENA = 17
ENB = 27

# Set up motor pins
GPIO.setup(IN1, GPIO.OUT)
GPIO.setup(IN2, GPIO.OUT)
GPIO.setup(IN3, GPIO.OUT)
GPIO.setup(IN4, GPIO.OUT)
GPIO.setup(ENA, GPIO.OUT)
GPIO.setup(ENB, GPIO.OUT)

# Set up PWM on Enable pins
pwmA = GPIO.PWM(ENA, 100)
pwmB = GPIO.PWM(ENB, 100)
pwmA.start(50)  # Start with 50% speed
pwmB.start(50)  # Start with 50% speed

# Define movement functions
def move_forward():
    GPIO.output(IN1, GPIO.HIGH)
    GPIO.output(IN2, GPIO.LOW)
    GPIO.output(IN3, GPIO.HIGH)
    GPIO.output(IN4, GPIO.LOW)


def move_backward():
```

```python
    GPIO.output(IN1, GPIO.LOW)
    GPIO.output(IN2, GPIO.HIGH)
    GPIO.output(IN3, GPIO.LOW)
    GPIO.output(IN4, GPIO.HIGH)

def turn_left():
    GPIO.output(IN1, GPIO.LOW)
    GPIO.output(IN2, GPIO.HIGH)
    GPIO.output(IN3, GPIO.HIGH)
    GPIO.output(IN4, GPIO.LOW)

def turn_right():
    GPIO.output(IN1, GPIO.HIGH)
    GPIO.output(IN2, GPIO.LOW)
    GPIO.output(IN3, GPIO.LOW)
    GPIO.output(IN4, GPIO.HIGH)

def stop():
    GPIO.output(IN1, GPIO.LOW)
    GPIO.output(IN2, GPIO.LOW)
    GPIO.output(IN3, GPIO.LOW)
    GPIO.output(IN4, GPIO.LOW)

# Main loop for continuous movement
try:
```

```python
while True:
    command = input("Enter command (w = forward, s = backward, a = left, d = right, x = stop, q = quit): ")

    if command == "w":
        print("Moving forward")
        move_forward()
        time.sleep(2)
        stop()
    elif command == "s":
        print("Moving backward")
        move_backward()
        time.sleep(2)
        stop()
    elif command == "a":
        print("Turning left")
        turn_left()
        time.sleep(1)
        stop()
    elif command == "d":
        print("Turning right")
        turn_right()
        time.sleep(1)
        stop()
    elif command == "x":
```

```
        print("Stopping")
        stop()
    elif command == "q":
        print("Exiting program")
        break
    else:
        print("Invalid command. Please use w, s, a, d, x, or
q.")
except KeyboardInterrupt:
    print("Program interrupted")
finally:
    stop()
    GPIO.cleanup()
    print("GPIO cleaned up")
```

3. Save and exit the file (**Ctrl + O**, **Enter**, then **Ctrl + X**).

Explanation of the Code

- **Movement Functions**: Each movement function (e.g., move_forward, move_backward) configures the GPIO pins to control the direction of the motors, creating the desired movement.

- **Control Loop**: The while loop allows the robot to keep moving based on user input. Each command (e.g., "w" for forward, "s" for backward) is executed for a specific duration, followed by a stop.

- **Stop Command**: Each movement is followed by a stop() command, ensuring the robot halts after the designated movement period.

Running the Program

1. Run the program by typing:

bash

python3 movement_control.py

2. **Controlling the Robot**:
   - ○ **w**: Moves the robot forward for 2 seconds.
   - ○ **s**: Moves the robot backward for 2 seconds.
   - ○ **a**: Turns the robot left for 1 second.
   - ○ **d**: Turns the robot right for 1 second.
   - ○ **x**: Stops the robot immediately.
   - ○ **q**: Exits the program.

Example: To move forward and then turn right, press "w", wait for the command to finish, and then press "d".

Enhancing the Control Loop

You can expand the control loop further by:

1. **Adding More Commands**: Try adding diagonal movements or in-place rotations to give the robot more flexibility.

2. **Adjusting Speeds Dynamically**: Use PWM to adjust motor speeds based on user input (e.g., "faster" or "slower").

3. **Loop with Sensor Input**: In later chapters, you'll learn to integrate sensor feedback to adapt the movement loop based on environmental data.

In this chapter, you learned to program basic movement patterns, introduced control loops to create continuous movement, and built a hands-on program that allows you to control the robot's movements using simple keyboard commands. With a control loop, the robot can execute commands continuously, which is essential for both manual and autonomous operation.

In the next chapter, we'll explore obstacle avoidance, adding sensors and logic that enable the robot to detect and avoid obstacles in its path. This will be a significant step toward making your robot more autonomous and interactive with its surroundings.

CHAPTER 12: INTRODUCING OBSTACLE AVOIDANCE

Obstacle avoidance is a key functionality in autonomous robotics, allowing the robot to navigate safely in its environment without colliding with objects. In this chapter, we'll introduce the concept of obstacle detection and avoidance, set up obstacle sensors, and connect them to the Raspberry Pi. You'll then write code to make your robot detect and avoid obstacles, enabling it to move independently within a controlled area.

The Concept of Obstacle Detection and Avoidance in Robotics

Obstacle avoidance enables a robot to detect and maneuver around obstacles to prevent collisions. This capability is especially useful in mobile robots, allowing them to navigate environments autonomously.

How Obstacle Avoidance Works:

1. **Sensor Detection**: Sensors like ultrasonic, infrared (IR), or LiDAR continuously monitor the area around the robot.

When an object is detected within a certain distance, the sensor signals the microcontroller (in this case, the Raspberry Pi).

2. **Decision Making**: Based on sensor data, the robot's program decides on the next movement. For example, if an obstacle is detected ahead, the robot might stop, turn, or choose a different path.

3. **Action Execution**: The robot executes the chosen movement, whether it's stopping, turning, or reversing, to avoid the obstacle and continue its journey.

Common Sensors for Obstacle Avoidance:

- **Ultrasonic Sensors**: Use sound waves to measure distance to nearby objects. They are effective for obstacle detection in a range of about 2cm to 400cm.
- **Infrared (IR) Sensors**: Emit infrared light and measure reflections. These are useful for short-range detection and line following.
- **LiDAR**: Provides high-accuracy distance measurements and can create a detailed map of the robot's surroundings, though it is more complex and costly.

For this chapter, we'll focus on using **ultrasonic sensors** to implement basic obstacle avoidance.

Setting Up Obstacle Sensors and Connecting Them to the Raspberry Pi

To implement obstacle avoidance, we'll use an **HC-SR04 ultrasonic sensor** to detect obstacles in front of the robot.

Materials Needed:

- 1 HC-SR04 ultrasonic sensor
- Breadboard and jumper wires
- Resistors (1kΩ and 2kΩ) for voltage divider

Wiring the Ultrasonic Sensor to the Raspberry Pi

1. **Power the Sensor**
   - Connect the **VCC** pin on the HC-SR04 to the **5V** pin on the Raspberry Pi.
   - Connect the **GND** pin on the HC-SR04 to a **GND** pin on the Raspberry Pi.

2. **Connect the TRIG and ECHO Pins**
   - Connect the **TRIG** pin of the HC-SR04 to **GPIO 23** on the Raspberry Pi.
   - Connect the **ECHO** pin to **GPIO 24** on the Raspberry Pi. Use a **voltage divider** with 1kΩ and 2kΩ resistors to step down the 5V signal from the ECHO pin to 3.3V, safe for the Raspberry Pi's GPIO input.

Voltage Divider Setup:

- Place a 2kΩ resistor between the ECHO pin and GPIO 24.
- Connect a 1kΩ resistor between GPIO 24 and GND.

Hands-on: Writing Code to Make the Robot Avoid Obstacles in Its Path

With the ultrasonic sensor connected, let's write a Python program to detect obstacles and command the robot to change direction when an obstacle is detected within a certain distance.

Step 1: Writing the Obstacle Avoidance Code

1. Open the Terminal and create a new Python file:

```bash
nano obstacle_avoidance.py
```

2. Write the following code to control the robot's movement and detect obstacles using the ultrasonic sensor:

```python
import RPi.GPIO as GPIO
import time

# Set up GPIO mode
```

```python
GPIO.setmode(GPIO.BCM)

# Define GPIO pins for motors
IN1 = 18
IN2 = 23
IN3 = 24
IN4 = 25
ENA = 17
ENB = 27

# Set up GPIO pins for ultrasonic sensor
TRIG = 23
ECHO = 24

# Set up motor pins
GPIO.setup(IN1, GPIO.OUT)
GPIO.setup(IN2, GPIO.OUT)
GPIO.setup(IN3, GPIO.OUT)
GPIO.setup(IN4, GPIO.OUT)
GPIO.setup(ENA, GPIO.OUT)
GPIO.setup(ENB, GPIO.OUT)

# Set up PWM on Enable pins
pwmA = GPIO.PWM(ENA, 100)
pwmB = GPIO.PWM(ENB, 100)
```

```python
pwmA.start(50)  # Start at 50% speed
pwmB.start(50)  # Start at 50% speed

# Set up ultrasonic sensor pins
GPIO.setup(TRIG, GPIO.OUT)
GPIO.setup(ECHO, GPIO.IN)

# Define movement functions
def move_forward():
    GPIO.output(IN1, GPIO.HIGH)
    GPIO.output(IN2, GPIO.LOW)
    GPIO.output(IN3, GPIO.HIGH)
    GPIO.output(IN4, GPIO.LOW)

def move_backward():
    GPIO.output(IN1, GPIO.LOW)
    GPIO.output(IN2, GPIO.HIGH)
    GPIO.output(IN3, GPIO.LOW)
    GPIO.output(IN4, GPIO.HIGH)

def turn_left():
    GPIO.output(IN1, GPIO.LOW)
    GPIO.output(IN2, GPIO.HIGH)
    GPIO.output(IN3, GPIO.HIGH)
    GPIO.output(IN4, GPIO.LOW)
```

```python
def turn_right():
    GPIO.output(IN1, GPIO.HIGH)
    GPIO.output(IN2, GPIO.LOW)
    GPIO.output(IN3, GPIO.LOW)
    GPIO.output(IN4, GPIO.HIGH)

def stop():
    GPIO.output(IN1, GPIO.LOW)
    GPIO.output(IN2, GPIO.LOW)
    GPIO.output(IN3, GPIO.LOW)
    GPIO.output(IN4, GPIO.LOW)

# Function to measure distance using ultrasonic sensor
def measure_distance():
    # Trigger a pulse
    GPIO.output(TRIG, True)
    time.sleep(0.00001)
    GPIO.output(TRIG, False)

    # Record start and end time of the pulse
    while GPIO.input(ECHO) == 0:
        start_time = time.time()
    while GPIO.input(ECHO) == 1:
        end_time = time.time()
```

```python
    # Calculate the distance
    duration = end_time - start_time
    distance = (duration * 34300) / 2  # Speed of sound is 34300 cm/s
    return distance


# Main loop for obstacle avoidance
try:
    while True:
        distance = measure_distance()
        print(f"Distance to obstacle: {distance:.2f} cm")

        if distance < 20:  # If obstacle is closer than 20 cm
            print("Obstacle detected! Turning...")
            stop()
            time.sleep(0.5)
            turn_right()  # Turn to avoid obstacle
            time.sleep(1)  # Adjust time for turning as needed
        else:
            print("Path is clear, moving forward")
            move_forward()
        time.sleep(0.1)
except KeyboardInterrupt:
    print("Program interrupted")
```

finally:

    stop()

    GPIO.cleanup()

    print("GPIO cleaned up")

3. Save and exit the file (**Ctrl + O, Enter, then Ctrl + X**).

Explanation of the Code

- **Distance Measurement**: The measure_distance() function sends a pulse to the ultrasonic sensor and calculates the time taken for the echo to return, which it then uses to determine the distance.
- **Control Loop**: The while loop continuously checks the distance to any object in front of the robot.
- **Obstacle Avoidance Logic**: If the detected distance is less than 20 cm, the robot stops and turns right to avoid the obstacle. Otherwise, it moves forward.

Running the Program

1. Run the program by typing:

bash

python3 obstacle_avoidance.py

2. **Testing Obstacle Avoidance**:

- o Place an object (like a box) in front of the robot to test its response. It should stop, turn, and then resume moving forward when the path is clear.
- o Adjust the distance threshold (20 cm in this example) as needed to fine-tune the robot's obstacle detection sensitivity.

Expanding the Obstacle Avoidance System

You can enhance this program further by:

- **Adding More Sensors**: Place ultrasonic or IR sensors on the sides and back of the robot for 360° obstacle detection.
- **Refining the Turning Mechanism**: Randomize or add logic to alternate turns (left and right) when avoiding obstacles.
- **Implementing Adaptive Speed**: Slow down the robot as it approaches an obstacle for smoother navigation.

In this chapter, you learned about obstacle avoidance in robotics, set up an ultrasonic sensor for detecting obstacles, and wrote a Python program to make your robot avoid objects in its path. With obstacle avoidance, your robot can now navigate independently, a fundamental capability in autonomous robotics.

In the next chapter, we'll introduce the line-following concept and program your robot to follow a designated path. Line-following is a popular application in robotics that further enhances the robot's autonomous capabilities by allowing it to navigate along predefined paths.

Chapter 13: Building a Line-Following Robot

Line-following is a popular task in robotics, where a robot is programmed to follow a designated path (usually a dark line on a light background) on a track. This chapter introduces line-following algorithms, sets up line-following sensors, and provides a hands-on guide to programming your robot to follow a line path. By the end of this chapter, your robot will be able to navigate a track autonomously by detecting and following a line.

Introduction to Line-Following Algorithms and Sensors

Line-following robots are widely used in autonomous navigation, warehouse automation, and educational robotics. They rely on sensors to detect a line and adjust the robot's movement accordingly.

How Line Following Works:

1. **Sensors**: Line-following robots typically use infrared (IR) sensors to detect the difference in color between a line and the surrounding area. For example, a black line on a white surface.

2. **Algorithm**: The robot constantly reads sensor values and uses them to determine its position relative to the line. Based on this input, the robot adjusts its direction to stay on the path.

3. **Control Mechanism**: The robot usually slows down or turns when it detects it's off the line, then repositions itself to stay centered on the line. This process is repeated continually to keep the robot on track.

Basic Line-Following Algorithms:

- **Simple Thresholding**: A basic approach where the robot turns slightly left or right when it detects the edge of the line.

- **Proportional Control (P-Controller)**: A more advanced approach that calculates the error between the robot's position and the line's center, allowing smoother movement.

For this chapter, we'll focus on a simple line-following algorithm to get the robot following a line path effectively.

Setting Up Line-Following Sensors on the Robot

To build a line-following robot, we'll use IR sensors to detect the line. You can use **QTR-1A** or **TCRT5000** IR sensors, which are commonly used in line-following robots.

Materials Needed:

- 2-3 IR sensors for line following
- Breadboard and jumper wires
- Electrical tape or black tape to create a line track on a light-colored surface

Wiring the IR Sensors to the Raspberry Pi

1. **Connecting Power to the IR Sensors**:
   o Connect the **VCC** pin of each IR sensor to the Raspberry Pi's **3.3V** or **5V** pin, depending on the sensor's operating voltage.
   o Connect the **GND** pin of each IR sensor to the Raspberry Pi's **GND**.

2. **Connecting Signal Pins**:
   o Connect each IR sensor's **OUT** pin to a separate GPIO pin on the Raspberry Pi to read the sensor values.
   o For this example:
     ▪ Connect the left IR sensor's OUT pin to **GPIO 16**.

- Connect the center IR sensor's OUT pin to **GPIO 20**.
- Connect the right IR sensor's OUT pin to **GPIO 21**.

Placing the Sensors:

- Mount the IR sensors near the front of the robot, positioning them close to the ground (a few millimeters above the track). Arrange them in a row: left, center, and right. The center sensor should be aligned directly over the line when the robot is centered.

Hands-on: Programming Your Robot to Follow a Line Path on a Track

Now that the sensors are set up, let's write a Python program that reads sensor values and controls the motors to keep the robot on the line.

Step 1: Writing the Line-Following Code

1. Open the Terminal on your Raspberry Pi and create a new Python file:

bash
nano line_follower.py

2. Write the following code to implement line following:

```python
python
import RPi.GPIO as GPIO
import time

# Set up GPIO mode
GPIO.setmode(GPIO.BCM)

# Define GPIO pins for motors
IN1 = 18
IN2 = 23
IN3 = 24
IN4 = 25
ENA = 17
ENB = 27

# Define GPIO pins for IR sensors
LEFT_SENSOR = 16
CENTER_SENSOR = 20
RIGHT_SENSOR = 21

# Set up motor pins
GPIO.setup(IN1, GPIO.OUT)
GPIO.setup(IN2, GPIO.OUT)
GPIO.setup(IN3, GPIO.OUT)
GPIO.setup(IN4, GPIO.OUT)
```

```python
GPIO.setup(ENA, GPIO.OUT)
GPIO.setup(ENB, GPIO.OUT)

# Set up PWM on Enable pins
pwmA = GPIO.PWM(ENA, 100)
pwmB = GPIO.PWM(ENB, 100)
pwmA.start(50)  # Start at 50% speed
pwmB.start(50)  # Start at 50% speed

# Set up IR sensor pins
GPIO.setup(LEFT_SENSOR, GPIO.IN)
GPIO.setup(CENTER_SENSOR, GPIO.IN)
GPIO.setup(RIGHT_SENSOR, GPIO.IN)

# Define movement functions
def move_forward():
    GPIO.output(IN1, GPIO.HIGH)
    GPIO.output(IN2, GPIO.LOW)
    GPIO.output(IN3, GPIO.HIGH)
    GPIO.output(IN4, GPIO.LOW)

def turn_left():
    GPIO.output(IN1, GPIO.LOW)
    GPIO.output(IN2, GPIO.LOW)
    GPIO.output(IN3, GPIO.HIGH)
```

```python
    GPIO.output(IN4, GPIO.LOW)

def turn_right():
    GPIO.output(IN1, GPIO.HIGH)
    GPIO.output(IN2, GPIO.LOW)
    GPIO.output(IN3, GPIO.LOW)
    GPIO.output(IN4, GPIO.LOW)

def stop():
    GPIO.output(IN1, GPIO.LOW)
    GPIO.output(IN2, GPIO.LOW)
    GPIO.output(IN3, GPIO.LOW)
    GPIO.output(IN4, GPIO.LOW)

# Main loop for line following
try:
    while True:
        # Read sensor values
        left_detected = GPIO.input(LEFT_SENSOR) == 0
        center_detected = GPIO.input(CENTER_SENSOR) == 0
        right_detected = GPIO.input(RIGHT_SENSOR) == 0

        # Line-following logic
        if center_detected:
```

```
        print("Line detected in center, moving forward")
        move_forward()
    elif left_detected:
        print("Line detected on left, turning left")
        turn_left()
    elif right_detected:
        print("Line detected on right, turning right")
        turn_right()
    else:
        print("No line detected, stopping")
        stop()

    time.sleep(0.1)
except KeyboardInterrupt:
    print("Program interrupted")
finally:
    stop()
    GPIO.cleanup()
    print("GPIO cleaned up")
```

3. Save and exit the file (**Ctrl + O, Enter**, then **Ctrl + X**).

Explanation of the Code

- **Sensor Readings**: The program reads the values from the three IR sensors. When the sensor detects a black line, it outputs a low signal (0), while a high signal (1) indicates a light surface.

- **Line-Following Logic**:
  o **Center Sensor Activated**: If the center sensor detects the line, the robot moves forward.
  o **Left Sensor Activated**: If only the left sensor detects the line, the robot turns left to get back on track.
  o **Right Sensor Activated**: If only the right sensor detects the line, the robot turns right to align with the path.
  o **No Line Detected**: If no sensors detect the line, the robot stops to prevent wandering off the track.

Running the Program

1. Run the program by typing:

bash

python3 line_follower.py

2. **Testing the Line-Following**:
   o Place the robot at the starting point of the track with the center sensor aligned over the line.

o Observe how the robot responds to curves and turns in the path. Adjust sensor positions and motor speeds if necessary to improve performance.

Fine-Tuning the Line-Following Behavior

After testing, you may find it helpful to make some adjustments:

1. **Adjust Sensor Position**: Position the sensors closer together or farther apart to improve line detection accuracy.
2. **Modify Turning Speed**: Use PWM to control the speed of turns for smoother line following, especially on curves.
3. **Enhance the Algorithm**: For a smoother and more responsive robot, consider implementing a proportional controller (P-controller) based on the error from the center line.

In this chapter, you learned about line-following algorithms and sensors, set up IR sensors for line detection, and programmed your robot to follow a line path using a basic algorithm. Line-following is a foundational skill in robotics, and with this setup, your robot can navigate simple tracks autonomously.

In the next chapter, we'll look at adding more advanced sensors or integrating multiple functionalities, making the robot even more versatile in its ability to navigate and interact with its environment.

This will further develop the autonomous capabilities you've started building with obstacle avoidance and line-following.

CHAPTER 14: ADDING A CAMERA FOR VISION PROCESSING

Adding a camera module to your robot opens up a range of possibilities for vision processing, enabling your robot to see and interpret its environment. In this chapter, we'll set up the Raspberry Pi Camera Module, capture and process images using Python and OpenCV, and display a live camera feed. By the end, you'll have the foundation to add vision-based capabilities to your robot, such as object recognition, color tracking, and more.

Setting Up the Raspberry Pi Camera Module

The Raspberry Pi Camera Module is a compact, high-quality camera that connects directly to the Raspberry Pi via the Camera Serial Interface (CSI) port. It's ideal for vision processing projects due to its compatibility and ease of use with the Pi.

Required Materials:

- Raspberry Pi Camera Module
- CSI cable (included with the camera module)

Step 1: Connecting the Camera Module

1. **Power off the Raspberry Pi** to avoid accidental damage.
2. Locate the **CSI camera connector** on the Raspberry Pi, typically located between the HDMI port and audio jack.
3. **Insert the CSI cable** from the camera module into the CSI connector:
   - Lift the plastic clip on the connector.
   - Insert the cable with the shiny contacts facing the Raspberry Pi's HDMI port.
   - Push the clip back down to secure the cable.

Step 2: Enabling the Camera Interface

1. **Boot up the Raspberry Pi** and open a Terminal.
2. Open the Raspberry Pi configuration tool:

```bash
sudo raspi-config
```

3. Navigate to **Interface Options** > **Camera** and select **Enable**.

4. Reboot the Raspberry Pi to apply the changes:

bash

sudo reboot

Step 3: Installing OpenCV for Image Processing

OpenCV (Open Source Computer Vision) is a popular library for image processing. If you don't have it installed, install OpenCV for Python:

bash

sudo apt update

sudo apt install python3-opencv

Capturing and Processing Images Using Python and OpenCV

With the camera module set up, let's start by capturing and displaying images using OpenCV. OpenCV's built-in functions allow us to capture images, process them, and display or save them to disk.

Basic Steps for Camera Capture:

1. Use OpenCV's VideoCapture function to access the camera feed.
2. Capture individual frames from the camera feed.
3. Display frames in a window using OpenCV's imshow function.

Hands-on: Writing Code to Display Live Camera Feed and Capture Images

Let's create a Python program that displays a live camera feed and captures images when prompted.

Step 1: Writing the Live Camera Feed Code

1. Open a Terminal on the Raspberry Pi and create a new Python file:

   bash
   nano camera_feed.py

2. Write the following code to access the camera feed and display it on the screen:

   python
   import cv2

   # Set up the camera
   camera = cv2.VideoCapture(0)   # 0 is the default camera ID

   if not camera.isOpened():
       print("Error: Could not access the camera.")
       exit()

```python
# Main loop to display live feed
try:
    while True:
        # Capture frame-by-frame
        ret, frame = camera.read()
        if not ret:
            print("Failed to grab frame")
            break

        # Display the resulting frame
        cv2.imshow("Live Camera Feed", frame)

        # Wait for the 'q' key to exit or 'c' key to capture an image
        key = cv2.waitKey(1)
        if key == ord('q'):
            print("Exiting live feed.")
            break
        elif key == ord('c'):
            # Capture and save the current frame as an image
            img_name = "captured_image.png"
            cv2.imwrite(img_name, frame)
            print(f"Image saved: {img_name}")

finally:
```

```
# Release the camera and close windows
camera.release()
cv2.destroyAllWindows()
```

3. Save and exit the file (**Ctrl + O, Enter**, then **Ctrl + X**).

Explanation of the Code:

- **Accessing the Camera**: VideoCapture(0) initializes the camera. If it's not detected, the program prints an error and exits.
- **Reading Frames**: The camera.read() function reads frames from the camera in real-time.
- **Displaying the Feed**: cv2.imshow() displays each frame in a window named "Live Camera Feed."
- **Keyboard Controls**:
  - Press **'q'** to exit the live feed.
  - Press **'c'** to capture an image and save it as "captured_image.png" in the current directory.

Running the Program

Run the program with:

bash
python3 camera_feed.py

1. **Testing the Live Feed**:

o You should see a live video feed displayed in a window.

o Press 'q' to close the window and exit the program.

o Press 'c' to capture an image, which will be saved as "captured_image.png".

2. **Troubleshooting Tips**:

o Ensure the camera is enabled in raspi-config.

o Verify the CSI cable is securely connected.

o If the video feed is not displaying, make sure OpenCV is installed correctly.

Expanding the Code for Basic Image Processing

With OpenCV, you can do much more than simply display the camera feed. Let's add some basic image processing to detect colors or edges in real-time.

1. Open the camera_feed.py file again:

bash

nano camera_feed.py

2. Modify the while loop to apply image processing effects:

python
Copy code
import cv2

```python
# Set up the camera
camera = cv2.VideoCapture(0)

if not camera.isOpened():
    print("Error: Could not access the camera.")
    exit()

try:
    while True:
        ret, frame = camera.read()
        if not ret:
            print("Failed to grab frame")
            break

        # Convert frame to grayscale
        gray_frame           =           cv2.cvtColor(frame,
cv2.COLOR_BGR2GRAY)

        # Apply edge detection
        edges = cv2.Canny(gray_frame, 50, 150)

        # Display original feed and processed feed
        cv2.imshow("Live Camera Feed", frame)
        cv2.imshow("Edge Detection Feed", edges)
```

```
key = cv2.waitKey(1)
if key == ord('q'):
    print("Exiting live feed.")
    break
elif key == ord('c'):
    img_name = "captured_image.png"
    cv2.imwrite(img_name, frame)
    print(f"Image saved: {img_name}")

finally:
    camera.release()
    cv2.destroyAllWindows()
```

3. Save and exit the file.

Explanation of Additional Code:

- **Grayscale Conversion**: cv2.cvtColor(frame, cv2.COLOR_BGR2GRAY) converts each frame to grayscale, simplifying edge detection.
- **Edge Detection**: cv2.Canny() performs edge detection on the grayscale frame. You can adjust the threshold values (50 and 150 in this case) to change the sensitivity.
- **Multiple Windows**: This code displays the original feed and a processed feed with edges detected.

Running the Enhanced Program

Run the enhanced code with:

bash

python3 camera_feed.py

You should now see two windows:

- **Live Camera Feed**: Shows the original video feed.
- **Edge Detection Feed**: Shows the edges detected in real time.

Expanding Vision Capabilities for Robotics

With OpenCV, you can add even more sophisticated vision processing to your robot:

1. **Object Recognition**: Use OpenCV's object recognition features to identify specific objects (e.g., circles or faces).
2. **Color Detection**: Program the robot to detect and follow specific colors, useful for tracking colored markers.
3. **Line Detection**: Use vision processing to detect and follow lines, an alternative to IR sensors for line-following robots.

In this chapter, you learned to set up the Raspberry Pi Camera Module, capture and display images, and use Python and OpenCV to add real-time image processing. You also created a program to display a live camera feed and capture images on command. These foundational skills open the door to more complex vision processing tasks, enabling your robot to interpret its surroundings visually.

In the next chapter, we'll explore more advanced vision processing techniques to enable your robot to recognize objects, detect colors, or even track movement. This will further enhance the robot's ability to interact with and respond to its environment.

CHAPTER 15: BASIC IMAGE PROCESSING FOR OBJECT DETECTION

Image processing techniques, such as edge detection, color tracking, and shape recognition, allow robots to interpret and respond to their surroundings. In this chapter, we'll introduce basic image processing concepts using OpenCV, a powerful open-source library for computer vision. We'll explore edge detection, color tracking, and shape recognition, and then create a hands-on example to detect specific objects or colors using Python and OpenCV.

Introduction to OpenCV and Basic Image Processing Techniques

OpenCV (Open Source Computer Vision) is a versatile library with a wide range of tools for image and video processing. Here are some core image processing techniques used in object detection:

1. **Edge Detection**
   - o **Purpose**: Edge detection identifies boundaries within an image, helping to distinguish objects and shapes.
   - o **Method**: The Canny edge detection algorithm is commonly used in OpenCV for its efficiency and accuracy.
2. **Color Tracking**
   - o **Purpose**: Color tracking is useful for detecting objects of specific colors, such as tracking a red ball or a green marker.
   - o **Method**: Convert the image to the HSV (Hue, Saturation, Value) color space, which makes it easier to filter colors. Then, use a mask to isolate the desired color.
3. **Shape Recognition**

- o **Purpose**: Shape recognition allows a robot to detect specific geometric shapes, such as circles, rectangles, or triangles.
- o **Method**: Find contours in the image and use contour approximation or shape-specific functions to detect shapes.

By combining these techniques, you can develop object detection systems that can recognize and respond to objects in real time.

Setting Up OpenCV for Image Processing

If you haven't installed OpenCV yet, follow these steps to ensure it's ready on your Raspberry Pi:

bash

sudo apt update

sudo apt install python3-opencv

You'll also need the Raspberry Pi Camera Module or a USB webcam for live video input, which we set up in Chapter 14.

Edge Detection, Color Tracking, and Shape Recognition

Each of these techniques can be implemented independently or combined depending on the application. Let's explore each in more detail.

1. **Edge Detection with Canny**

Edge detection is the process of finding and highlighting the boundaries of objects in an image. The **Canny Edge Detection** algorithm is popular due to its effectiveness and simplicity in OpenCV.

```python
python
# Convert to grayscale
gray_frame                =                cv2.cvtColor(frame,
cv2.COLOR_BGR2GRAY)


# Apply Canny edge detection
edges = cv2.Canny(gray_frame, 50, 150)    # Adjust
thresholds as needed
```

2. **Color Tracking in HSV Color Space**

Color tracking identifies objects based on color, which is helpful for detecting colored markers or objects. The HSV color space separates color information, making it easier to define specific color ranges.

```python
python
# Convert the image to HSV color space
hsv_frame                =                cv2.cvtColor(frame,
cv2.COLOR_BGR2HSV)


# Define color range for tracking (e.g., red)
```

lower_red = (160, 100, 100)

upper_red = (180, 255, 255)

\# Create a mask for the red color

mask = cv2.inRange(hsv_frame, lower_red, upper_red)

3. **Shape Recognition with Contours**

Shape recognition involves finding and approximating contours to identify geometric shapes. For example, circles, rectangles, and triangles can be recognized based on their contours.

python

\# Convert to grayscale and apply thresholding

gray_frame = cv2.cvtColor(frame, cv2.COLOR_BGR2GRAY)

_, thresh = cv2.threshold(gray_frame, 127, 255, cv2.THRESH_BINARY)

\# Find contours in the thresholded image

contours, _ = cv2.findContours(thresh, cv2.RETR_TREE, cv2.CHAIN_APPROX_SIMPLE)

\# Loop through contours and approximate shapes

for contour in contours:

```python
approx = cv2.approxPolyDP(contour, 0.02 *
cv2.arcLength(contour, True), True)
    if len(approx) == 3:
        shape = "Triangle"
    elif len(approx) == 4:
        shape = "Rectangle"
    elif len(approx) > 4:
        shape = "Circle"
```

Hands-on: Writing Code to Detect Specific Objects or Colors

Let's combine these techniques to create a program that can detect specific colors or shapes in real time.

Step 1: Writing the Object Detection Code

1. Open the Terminal and create a new Python file:

```bash
bash
nano object_detection.py
```

2. Write the following code to capture video, detect edges, track a color, and recognize shapes:

```python
python
import cv2
import numpy as np
```

```python
# Set up the camera
camera = cv2.VideoCapture(0)

if not camera.isOpened():
    print("Error: Could not access the camera.")
    exit()

try:
    while True:
        # Capture frame-by-frame
        ret, frame = camera.read()
        if not ret:
            print("Failed to grab frame")
            break

        # Edge Detection
        gray_frame          =          cv2.cvtColor(frame,
cv2.COLOR_BGR2GRAY)
        edges = cv2.Canny(gray_frame, 50, 150)

        # Color Tracking (e.g., red)
        hsv_frame           =          cv2.cvtColor(frame,
cv2.COLOR_BGR2HSV)
        lower_red = (160, 100, 100)
        upper_red = (180, 255, 255)
```

```python
color_mask = cv2.inRange(hsv_frame, lower_red,
upper_red)
color_detected = cv2.bitwise_and(frame, frame,
mask=color_mask)

# Shape Recognition
_, thresh = cv2.threshold(gray_frame, 127, 255,
cv2.THRESH_BINARY)
contours, _ = cv2.findContours(thresh,
cv2.RETR_TREE, cv2.CHAIN_APPROX_SIMPLE)
for contour in contours:
    approx = cv2.approxPolyDP(contour, 0.02 *
cv2.arcLength(contour, True), True)
    x, y, w, h = cv2.boundingRect(approx)

    if len(approx) == 3:
        shape = "Triangle"
    elif len(approx) == 4:
        shape = "Rectangle"
    elif len(approx) > 4:
        shape = "Circle"
    else:
        shape = None

    # Draw shapes on the frame
```

```
    if shape:
        cv2.putText(frame,    shape,    (x,   y   -   10),
cv2.FONT_HERSHEY_SIMPLEX, 0.5, (255, 255, 255), 2)
        cv2.drawContours(frame, [approx], 0, (0, 255, 0),
2)


    # Display the feeds
    cv2.imshow("Live Feed", frame)
    cv2.imshow("Edge Detection", edges)
    cv2.imshow("Color Tracking", color_detected)


    # Press 'q' to quit
    if cv2.waitKey(1) & 0xFF == ord('q'):
        break

finally:
    # Release the camera and close all windows
    camera.release()
    cv2.destroyAllWindows()
```

3. Save and exit the file (**Ctrl + O, Enter,** then **Ctrl + X**).

Explanation of the Code:

- **Edge Detection**: We use Canny edge detection to highlight edges in the live feed, which is displayed in a separate window.

- **Color Tracking**: We isolate a color (red in this example) using a mask in the HSV color space and display the masked color.

- **Shape Recognition**: We detect contours in the frame, approximate their shapes, and label recognized shapes (triangle, rectangle, circle) in the live feed.

Running the Object Detection Program

1. Run the program with:

   bash
   python3 object_detection.py

2. **Testing Object Detection**:
   - Observe the **Live Feed** window, where detected shapes are labeled.
   - Check the **Edge Detection** window for a view of the edges.
   - The **Color Tracking** window shows only the tracked color (red in this case).

3. **Adjusting for Different Colors and Shapes**:

- o Change the lower_red and upper_red HSV values to track other colors.
- o Experiment with different shapes by placing simple geometric objects in view and observing the shape detection in the live feed.

Applications and Extensions

With basic object detection in place, you can further explore:

- **Object Recognition with Machine Learning**: Use pre-trained models to detect and classify complex objects.
- **Real-time Tracking**: Combine color and shape detection for dynamic tracking (e.g., following a colored ball).
- **Pattern Recognition**: Use shape and color patterns to recognize symbols or markers for navigation.

In this chapter, you explored the basics of object detection using OpenCV, covering edge detection, color tracking, and shape recognition. You created a hands-on program to detect specific colors and shapes in real-time, enhancing your robot's ability to perceive and interact with its environment.

In the next chapter, we'll introduce more advanced object recognition techniques, such as using machine learning models, to enable your robot to recognize complex objects and make more intelligent decisions based on visual data.

CHAPTER 16: IMPLEMENTING OBJECT TRACKING

Object tracking is a valuable technique in robotics, enabling a robot to detect and follow specific objects, such as people, markers, or items of a particular color. In this chapter, we'll introduce the concept of object tracking, discuss its applications, and write code to track a colored object in real-time using the Raspberry Pi Camera Module and OpenCV. By the end, your robot will be able to detect and follow a specific object, opening up possibilities for applications like automated surveillance, interactive robots, and more.

Introduction to Object Tracking and Its Applications in Robotics

Object tracking is a computer vision technique that involves detecting an object in a video feed and continuously monitoring its position over time. The ability to track objects gives robots a powerful capability to interact intelligently with their surroundings.

Applications of Object Tracking:

1. **Human-Following Robots**: Object tracking can be used to follow people, making it ideal for assistance robots.
2. **Color-Based Object Tracking**: Tracking objects based on color is useful in applications like ball-following robots or tracking specific markers.

3. **Security and Surveillance**: Robots with tracking capabilities can monitor areas, detect intruders, or follow specific targets.

4. **Interactive Robots**: Object tracking adds interactivity, allowing robots to respond to gestures, movement, or visual signals from the environment.

In this chapter, we'll focus on color-based object tracking to help the robot follow a specific colored object, such as a ball or marker.

Programming Your Robot to Detect and Follow a Specific Object

The simplest approach to object tracking in a robotics context is to use color-based tracking, which involves:

1. **Detecting the Object**: Use color thresholds in the HSV color space to identify the desired object.

2. **Determining Position and Movement**: Find the object's position within the frame and calculate any movement needed to keep it centered.

3. **Controlling the Robot**: Based on the object's position, issue commands to the robot to move forward, turn, or adjust its direction to stay aligned with the target.

Key Concepts:

- **HSV Color Space**: The HSV (Hue, Saturation, Value) color space makes it easier to isolate specific colors and is more robust against lighting variations compared to the RGB color space.

- **Contour Detection**: Once we isolate the color, we use contours to find the object's position within the frame.
- **Movement Logic**: Based on the object's position, the robot can adjust its movement to keep the object centered.

Hands-on: Writing Code to Track a Colored Object with the Camera

Let's write a Python program that captures live video, detects a colored object, and controls the robot to follow the object.

Materials Needed:

- Raspberry Pi with Camera Module or USB webcam
- Object to track (such as a colored ball or marker)
- Raspberry Pi robot with wheels and motor control (setup from previous chapters)

Step 1: Writing the Object Tracking Code

1. Open a Terminal on the Raspberry Pi and create a new Python file:

bash

nano object_tracking.py

2. Write the following code to capture video, detect the colored object, and control the robot based on the object's position:

```python
import cv2
import numpy as np
import RPi.GPIO as GPIO
import time

# Set up GPIO mode
GPIO.setmode(GPIO.BCM)

# Motor control pins
IN1 = 18
IN2 = 23
IN3 = 24
IN4 = 25
ENA = 17
ENB = 27

# Set up motor pins
GPIO.setup(IN1, GPIO.OUT)
GPIO.setup(IN2, GPIO.OUT)
GPIO.setup(IN3, GPIO.OUT)
GPIO.setup(IN4, GPIO.OUT)
```

```python
GPIO.setup(ENA, GPIO.OUT)
GPIO.setup(ENB, GPIO.OUT)

# Set up PWM on Enable pins
pwmA = GPIO.PWM(ENA, 100)
pwmB = GPIO.PWM(ENB, 100)
pwmA.start(50)  # Start with 50% speed
pwmB.start(50)  # Start with 50% speed

# Define movement functions
def move_forward():
    GPIO.output(IN1, GPIO.HIGH)
    GPIO.output(IN2, GPIO.LOW)
    GPIO.output(IN3, GPIO.HIGH)
    GPIO.output(IN4, GPIO.LOW)

def turn_left():
    GPIO.output(IN1, GPIO.LOW)
    GPIO.output(IN2, GPIO.LOW)
    GPIO.output(IN3, GPIO.HIGH)
    GPIO.output(IN4, GPIO.LOW)

def turn_right():
    GPIO.output(IN1, GPIO.HIGH)
    GPIO.output(IN2, GPIO.LOW)
```

```python
    GPIO.output(IN3, GPIO.LOW)
    GPIO.output(IN4, GPIO.LOW)

def stop():
    GPIO.output(IN1, GPIO.LOW)
    GPIO.output(IN2, GPIO.LOW)
    GPIO.output(IN3, GPIO.LOW)
    GPIO.output(IN4, GPIO.LOW)

# Set up the camera
camera = cv2.VideoCapture(0)
if not camera.isOpened():
    print("Error: Could not access the camera.")
    exit()

try:
    while True:
        # Capture frame-by-frame
        ret, frame = camera.read()
        if not ret:
            print("Failed to grab frame")
            break

        # Convert frame to HSV
```

```python
hsv_frame                =              cv2.cvtColor(frame,
cv2.COLOR_BGR2HSV)

# Define color range for tracking (e.g., blue object)
lower_blue = (100, 150, 50)
upper_blue = (140, 255, 255)

# Create a mask for the color
mask    =    cv2.inRange(hsv_frame,    lower_blue,
upper_blue)

# Find contours in the mask
contours,    _    =    cv2.findContours(mask,
cv2.RETR_TREE, cv2.CHAIN_APPROX_SIMPLE)
if contours:
    # Find the largest contour
    largest_contour            =            max(contours,
key=cv2.contourArea)
    (x, y, w, h) = cv2.boundingRect(largest_contour)
    cx = x + w // 2  # Center x of the object
    cy = y + h // 2  # Center y of the object

    # Draw a rectangle around the object
    cv2.rectangle(frame, (x, y), (x + w, y + h), (0, 255,
0), 2)
```

```
            # Determine movement based on object's position
            frame_center = frame.shape[1] // 2
            if cx < frame_center - 50:
                print("Turning left")
                turn_left()
            elif cx > frame_center + 50:
                print("Turning right")
                turn_right()
            else:
                print("Moving forward")
                move_forward()
        else:
            # Stop if no object is detected
            print("Object not detected, stopping")
            stop()

        # Display the frame
        cv2.imshow("Object Tracking", frame)

        # Exit on 'q' key
        if cv2.waitKey(1) & 0xFF == ord('q'):
            break

finally:
```

```
stop()
GPIO.cleanup()
camera.release()
cv2.destroyAllWindows()
```

3. Save and exit the file (**Ctrl + O**, **Enter**, then **Ctrl + X**).

Explanation of the Code:

- **Color Masking**: The code uses the HSV color space to isolate a blue object within the defined color range.
- **Contour Detection**: The program finds the largest contour, assumes it's the target object, and calculates the object's center (cx).
- **Movement Logic**: Based on the object's position within the frame, the robot adjusts its movement:
    - If the object is on the left, the robot turns left.
    - If the object is on the right, the robot turns right.
    - If the object is centered, the robot moves forward.

Running the Object Tracking Program

1. Run the program:

bash

python3 object_tracking.py

2. **Testing Object Tracking**:

   o Place a blue object in the camera's view.

   o As you move the object left or right, the robot should adjust its direction to keep the object centered.

   o The robot will move forward as long as the object stays centered and stop if it's lost.

3. **Modifying for Different Colors**:

   o Adjust the lower_blue and upper_blue HSV values to track different colors. You can use tools like the OpenCV Color Picker to find the HSV range for your target color.

Expanding Object Tracking Capabilities

With basic object tracking set up, here are ways to expand this project:

1. **Dynamic Object Size Tracking**: Adjust the robot's speed based on the object's distance (e.g., faster when the object is farther).

2. **Multiple Object Detection**: Track more than one object by adding color masks for each target.

3. **Gesture Tracking**: Detect specific shapes or movements as gestures and respond accordingly.

In this chapter, you learned how to implement basic object tracking using color-based detection. You wrote a program that enables your robot to detect, follow, and track an object based on color, making it capable of responding dynamically to changes in its environment. Object tracking is a valuable skill in robotics, useful for applications like human-following robots, interactive robots, and automation.

In the next chapter, we'll delve into advanced vision processing techniques, including pre-trained object recognition models. These will allow your robot to identify specific objects and make more sophisticated decisions based on complex visual data.

CHAPTER 17: INTRODUCING ARTIFICIAL INTELLIGENCE IN ROBOTICS

Artificial intelligence (AI) and machine learning (ML) bring powerful capabilities to robotics, enabling robots to recognize patterns, learn from experience, and make more complex decisions. In this chapter, we'll introduce the basics of AI and ML, discuss their applications in robotics, and set up a basic AI model to recognize simple objects. By the end, you'll understand how AI can enhance a robot's functionality and gain hands-on experience with a simple object recognition model.

Basics of AI and Machine Learning in the Context of Robotics

AI in robotics enables a robot to perceive, process, and act on information in more sophisticated ways than rule-based programming alone. Machine learning, a subset of AI, allows a robot to learn from data, recognize patterns, and improve over time.

Core Concepts in AI and ML for Robotics:

1. **Artificial Intelligence (AI)**: AI refers to the simulation of human intelligence in machines, allowing them to perform tasks that usually require human intelligence, like

recognizing objects, making decisions, or understanding language.

2. **Machine Learning (ML)**: ML involves training algorithms on data to recognize patterns or make predictions. In robotics, ML is used to identify objects, predict actions, and adapt to dynamic environments.

3. **Deep Learning**: A branch of ML, deep learning uses neural networks with many layers to model complex patterns in data, such as images or sounds. Deep learning has enabled major advances in computer vision, enabling robots to recognize complex objects, people, or gestures.

Applications of AI in Robotics:

- **Object Recognition**: AI models can recognize and classify objects, enabling robots to identify items in their environment, such as tools, landmarks, or faces.

- **Speech and Gesture Recognition**: Robots can understand verbal or non-verbal cues, enabling more natural interaction with humans.

- **Path Planning and Navigation**: ML algorithms can analyze sensor data to navigate complex environments, avoiding obstacles and finding the most efficient path.

Overview of Simple Machine Learning Models for Robotics Applications

Before diving into complex deep learning models, let's explore a few simple machine learning models that are suitable for robotics:

1. **Classification Models**:
   - **Purpose**: Classify inputs into categories, such as identifying if an object is a "cup" or "book."
   - **Example Algorithms**: Support Vector Machines (SVM), K-Nearest Neighbors (KNN), and Logistic Regression.

2. **Object Detection Models**:
   - **Purpose**: Not only classify objects but also locate them within an image.
   - **Example Models**: Models like MobileNet or SSD (Single Shot MultiBox Detector) can detect multiple objects in a scene with bounding boxes.

3. **Clustering Models**:
   - **Purpose**: Group similar items based on features, useful for tasks like segmenting a scene or categorizing objects.
   - **Example Algorithms**: K-Means Clustering.

Using Pre-trained Models: Training deep learning models from scratch requires significant data and computational resources, which can be challenging on a Raspberry Pi. Instead, we can use pre-trained models for common tasks like object detection or classification, which are efficient and easy to implement.

Hands-on: Setting Up a Basic AI Model to Recognize Simple Objects

For this hands-on project, we'll use a pre-trained model with **TensorFlow** and **OpenCV** to recognize simple objects in real-time. We'll use MobileNet, a lightweight model that can identify hundreds of common objects and works well on devices with limited processing power.

Materials Needed:

- Raspberry Pi with Camera Module or USB webcam
- TensorFlow and OpenCV installed on the Raspberry Pi

Step 1: Installing TensorFlow and Necessary Libraries

If you haven't installed TensorFlow yet, you can install it using:

bash

pip3 install tensorflow

Ensure that OpenCV is installed, as we'll be using it to process the camera feed:

bash

sudo apt update

sudo apt install python3-opencv

Step 2: Downloading the Pre-trained MobileNet Model

The MobileNet model is available as part of TensorFlow's pre-trained models for object detection.

1. **Download the MobileNet SSD model**:
    - Create a new directory for the model:

      bash
      mkdir ~/models && cd ~/models

    - Download the MobileNet SSD model with the following command:

      bash
      wget
      https://storage.googleapis.com/download.tensorflow
      .org/models/tflite/coco_ssd_mobilenet_v1_1.0_qua
      nt_2018_06_29.zip

    - Unzip the model files:

      bash
      unzip
      coco_ssd_mobilenet_v1_1.0_quant_2018_06_29.zi
      p

2. **Load the Model in Python**: We'll use TensorFlow Lite to load and run the MobileNet model.

Step 3: Writing the Object Recognition Code

Let's create a Python program that uses the MobileNet model to recognize objects in real-time from the camera feed.

1. Open a Terminal and create a new Python file:

   bash
   nano object_recognition.py

2. Write the following code to load the model, capture the camera feed, and detect objects:

   python
   ```python
   import cv2
   import numpy as np
   import tensorflow as tf

   # Load the TFLite model and allocate tensors
   model_path = "~/models/detect.tflite"
   interpreter = tf.lite.Interpreter(model_path=model_path)
   interpreter.allocate_tensors()

   # Get input and output details
   ```

```python
input_details = interpreter.get_input_details()
output_details = interpreter.get_output_details()

# Load the labels file
labels = []
with open("coco_labels.txt", "r") as file:
    labels = [line.strip() for line in file.readlines()]

# Set up the camera
camera = cv2.VideoCapture(0)
if not camera.isOpened():
    print("Error: Could not access the camera.")
    exit()

# Define helper function for object detection
def detect_objects(frame):
    input_shape = input_details[0]['shape']
    frame_resized = cv2.resize(frame, (input_shape[2], input_shape[1]))
    input_data = np.expand_dims(frame_resized, axis=0)

    # Run the model on the input image
    interpreter.set_tensor(input_details[0]['index'], input_data)
    interpreter.invoke()
```

```
# Get the results
boxes                                    =
interpreter.get_tensor(output_details[0]['index'])[0]
    class_ids                            =
interpreter.get_tensor(output_details[1]['index'])[0]
    scores                               =
interpreter.get_tensor(output_details[2]['index'])[0]

# Process the results
height, width, _ = frame.shape
for i in range(len(scores)):
    if scores[i] > 0.5:
        ymin, xmin, ymax, xmax = boxes[i]
        x1, y1, x2, y2 = int(xmin * width), int(ymin *
height), int(xmax * width), int(ymax * height)
        label = labels[int(class_ids[i])]
        confidence = scores[i]

        # Draw the bounding box and label
        cv2.rectangle(frame, (x1, y1), (x2, y2), (0, 255, 0),
2)
        cv2.putText(frame, f"{label}: {confidence:.2f}",
(x1, y1 - 10), cv2.FONT_HERSHEY_SIMPLEX, 0.5, (0,
255, 0), 2)
```

```
        return frame

    try:
        while True:
            # Capture frame-by-frame
            ret, frame = camera.read()
            if not ret:
                print("Failed to grab frame")
                break

            # Detect objects in the frame
            frame = detect_objects(frame)

            # Display the frame
            cv2.imshow("Object Recognition", frame)

            # Exit on 'q' key
            if cv2.waitKey(1) & 0xFF == ord('q'):
                break

    finally:
        camera.release()
        cv2.destroyAllWindows()
```

3. Save and exit the file (**Ctrl + O**, **Enter**, then **Ctrl + X**).

Explanation of the Code:

- **Loading the Model**: The code loads the MobileNet SSD model with TensorFlow Lite and prepares it for inference.
- **Object Detection**: The detect_objects function resizes each frame to the model's input size, runs inference, and retrieves the bounding boxes, class IDs, and confidence scores.
- **Displaying Results**: For each detected object, the program draws a bounding box and displays the object label and confidence score.

Running the Object Recognition Program

1. Run the program:

   bash

   Copy code

   python3 object_recognition.py

2. **Testing Object Recognition**:
   - You should see a live video feed with bounding boxes and labels over detected objects.
   - The model can recognize common objects like "person," "car," "bottle," etc.
   - Press 'q' to exit the program.

Expanding AI Capabilities in Robotics

With a basic AI model running on your robot, consider expanding its capabilities:

1. **Real-time Tracking and Follow**: Integrate object recognition with tracking to have your robot follow recognized objects.

2. **Gesture and Pose Recognition**: Use models to recognize gestures, allowing users to control the robot with hand signals.

3. **Speech and Sound Recognition**: Incorporate other forms of AI, like speech recognition, to add multi-modal interactions.

In this chapter, you explored the basics of AI and machine learning in robotics, learned about simple ML models, and implemented a pre-trained MobileNet model to recognize objects in real-time. This opens up many possibilities for your robot to interpret and respond to its environment more intelligently.

In the next chapter, we'll look into advanced AI and ML techniques, such as custom model training and deeper integration of AI with robotic functionalities, allowing for even more complex behaviors and applications.

CHAPTER 18: VOICE CONTROL FOR YOUR ROBOT

Voice control is an exciting addition to robotics, allowing users to command the robot using spoken words. In this chapter, we'll introduce speech recognition on the Raspberry Pi, set up a microphone, and configure voice recognition software. You'll learn to program basic voice commands to control your robot's movements, giving it a more interactive and user-friendly interface.

Introduction to Speech Recognition on the Raspberry Pi

Speech recognition converts spoken language into text, which the robot can interpret to perform specific tasks. In robotics, voice control enhances usability, making robots more accessible and enabling hands-free control.

Applications of Voice Control in Robotics:

1. **Hands-Free Navigation**: Commanding the robot to move forward, backward, or stop.

2. **Complex Command Sequences**: Enabling robots to perform multiple actions based on specific commands, like "start patrol" or "follow me."

3. **Interactive Applications**: Robots that can respond to questions or follow simple instructions, making them more interactive.

To add voice control, we'll use **SpeechRecognition**, a Python library compatible with the Google Speech Recognition API, which is a free and widely used option for simple voice commands.

Setting Up a Microphone and Configuring Voice Recognition Software

To implement voice control, we'll first set up a microphone with the Raspberry Pi and install the necessary software for voice recognition.

Required Materials:

- USB microphone (or compatible microphone with the Raspberry Pi's audio input)

Step 1: Setting Up the Microphone

1. **Connect the Microphone**: Insert the USB microphone into a USB port on the Raspberry Pi.

2. **Verify Microphone Connection**:
   - Open a Terminal and list the audio input devices:

bash

arecord -l

- o You should see the microphone listed as a **capture** device. If it's detected, make a note of its device number (e.g., hw:1,0).

3. **Test the Microphone**:
   - o Record a short audio sample to confirm the microphone works:

bash

arecord --device=hw:1,0 -d 5 -f cd test.wav

- o Play back the recorded file to verify:

bash

aplay test.wav

Step 2: Installing Speech Recognition Software

1. **Install the SpeechRecognition Library**:

bash

pip3 install SpeechRecognition

2. **Install PyAudio for Microphone Support**:
   - o PyAudio enables the microphone to work with SpeechRecognition.

bash

sudo apt update

sudo apt install python3-pyaudio

○ If you encounter issues with PyAudio, you can also try installing it via pip:

bash

pip3 install pyaudio

Hands-on: Programming Voice Commands to Control Your Robot's Movements

With the microphone and software set up, we can now write a program that listens for specific voice commands and translates them into movement instructions for the robot.

Voice Commands: We'll start with a few simple commands:

- **"forward"**: Move the robot forward
- **"backward"**: Move the robot backward
- **"left"**: Turn left
- **"right"**: Turn right
- **"stop"**: Stop the robot

Step 1: Writing the Voice Control Code

1. Open a Terminal and create a new Python file:

bash

nano voice_control.py

2. Write the following code to recognize voice commands and control the robot:

```python
import speech_recognition as sr
import RPi.GPIO as GPIO
import time

# Set up GPIO mode
GPIO.setmode(GPIO.BCM)

# Motor control pins
IN1 = 18
IN2 = 23
IN3 = 24
IN4 = 25
ENA = 17
ENB = 27

# Set up motor pins
GPIO.setup(IN1, GPIO.OUT)
GPIO.setup(IN2, GPIO.OUT)
GPIO.setup(IN3, GPIO.OUT)
```

```
GPIO.setup(IN4, GPIO.OUT)
GPIO.setup(ENA, GPIO.OUT)
GPIO.setup(ENB, GPIO.OUT)

# Set up PWM on Enable pins
pwmA = GPIO.PWM(ENA, 100)
pwmB = GPIO.PWM(ENB, 100)
pwmA.start(50)  # Start with 50% speed
pwmB.start(50)  # Start with 50% speed

# Define movement functions
def move_forward():
    GPIO.output(IN1, GPIO.HIGH)
    GPIO.output(IN2, GPIO.LOW)
    GPIO.output(IN3, GPIO.HIGH)
    GPIO.output(IN4, GPIO.LOW)


def move_backward():
    GPIO.output(IN1, GPIO.LOW)
    GPIO.output(IN2, GPIO.HIGH)
    GPIO.output(IN3, GPIO.LOW)
    GPIO.output(IN4, GPIO.HIGH)


def turn_left():
    GPIO.output(IN1, GPIO.LOW)
```

```python
    GPIO.output(IN2, GPIO.LOW)
    GPIO.output(IN3, GPIO.HIGH)
    GPIO.output(IN4, GPIO.LOW)

def turn_right():
    GPIO.output(IN1, GPIO.HIGH)
    GPIO.output(IN2, GPIO.LOW)
    GPIO.output(IN3, GPIO.LOW)
    GPIO.output(IN4, GPIO.LOW)

def stop():
    GPIO.output(IN1, GPIO.LOW)
    GPIO.output(IN2, GPIO.LOW)
    GPIO.output(IN3, GPIO.LOW)
    GPIO.output(IN4, GPIO.LOW)

# Initialize the recognizer
recognizer = sr.Recognizer()

# Main loop to listen for voice commands
try:
    with sr.Microphone() as source:
        print("Adjusting for ambient noise...")
        recognizer.adjust_for_ambient_noise(source)
        print("Listening for commands...")
```

```python
while True:
    # Listen for a command
    audio = recognizer.listen(source)

    try:
        # Recognize the command
        command = recognizer.recognize_google(audio).lower()
        print(f"Command received: {command}")

        # Execute movement based on command
        if "forward" in command:
            print("Moving forward")
            move_forward()
            time.sleep(1)
            stop()
        elif "backward" in command:
            print("Moving backward")
            move_backward()
            time.sleep(1)
            stop()
        elif "left" in command:
            print("Turning left")
            turn_left()
```

```python
            time.sleep(1)
            stop()
        elif "right" in command:
            print("Turning right")
            turn_right()
            time.sleep(1)
            stop()
        elif "stop" in command:
            print("Stopping")
            stop()
        elif "exit" in command:
            print("Exiting voice control")
            break

    except sr.UnknownValucError:
        print("Could not understand the command")
    except sr.RequestError:
        print("Error with the speech recognition service")

except KeyboardInterrupt:
    print("Program interrupted")
finally:
    stop()
    GPIO.cleanup()
    print("GPIO cleaned up")
```

3. Save and exit the file (**Ctrl + O**, **Enter**, then **Ctrl + X**).

Explanation of the Code:

- **Speech Recognition**: The program uses recognizer.listen(source) to listen for voice commands and recognizer.recognize_google(audio) to convert audio to text.
- **Command Processing**: Based on the recognized text, the program calls different movement functions to control the robot.
- **Error Handling**: If the speech recognizer fails to understand or if there's an issue with the service, it catches the error and continues listening.

Running the Voice Control Program

1. Run the program with:

   bash
   python3 voice_control.py

2. **Testing Voice Commands**:
   - Speak commands like "forward," "backward," "left," "right," and "stop."
   - The robot should respond to each command with the corresponding movement.

- o To exit the program, say "exit" or press **Ctrl + C** in the Terminal.

3. **Troubleshooting Tips**:
    - o If the robot doesn't respond, ensure the microphone is correctly configured and test it with simple audio recording.
    - o Adjust for ambient noise if the recognition isn't accurate by saying "adjusting for ambient noise..." at the start of the program.

Expanding Voice Control Capabilities

Once you have basic voice control working, here are some ways to expand:

1. **Additional Commands**: Add more commands, like "faster," "slower," "start patrol," or "follow."
2. **Phrase Recognition**: Use phrases like "turn left slowly" or "move forward quickly" for more nuanced control.
3. **Multi-language Support**: Google Speech Recognition supports multiple languages, enabling control in different languages.
4. **Feedback Mechanisms**: Have the robot confirm actions with LEDs, sounds, or a display to provide feedback.

In this chapter, you learned to set up voice control for your robot using a microphone, the SpeechRecognition library, and basic

Python code. By integrating speech recognition, you've created an interactive and user-friendly way to control your robot, opening doors to hands-free applications.

In the next chapter, we'll explore advanced AI integration to allow the robot to recognize complex phrases, provide more sophisticated responses, and potentially even interact in a conversation. This will further enhance the robot's ability to respond and adapt to human input.

CHAPTER 19: ADDING WI-FI CONTROL WITH A WEB INTERFACE

In this chapter, we'll introduce Wi-Fi-based remote control for your robot by creating a web interface. A web interface provides a convenient and accessible way to control the robot from any device with a browser, such as a smartphone, tablet, or computer. We'll set up Wi-Fi on the Raspberry Pi, build a simple web interface using Flask, and create a live control panel with buttons for movement. By the end, you'll have a remote control solution for your robot that works over a local network.

Setting Up Wi-Fi on the Raspberry Pi for Remote Control

First, we need to ensure that the Raspberry Pi is connected to Wi-Fi. This allows it to host a web server, enabling other devices on the same network to connect and control the robot.

Step 1: Connecting the Raspberry Pi to Wi-Fi

1. **Check Wi-Fi Connection**: If the Raspberry Pi is not yet connected to Wi-Fi, go to the Raspberry Pi's Desktop and click the network icon in the top-right corner. Select your Wi-Fi network and enter the password.

2. **Verify the IP Address**:

    ○ Open a Terminal and use the following command to check the IP address:

    bash

    hostname -I

    ○ Make a note of the IP address (e.g., 192.168.1.100). This address will be used to access the web interface.

Step 2: Installing Flask

Flask is a lightweight Python web framework that makes it easy to create web applications.

1. Install Flask on the Raspberry Pi:

    bash

    pip3 install flask

Building a Simple Web Interface Using Flask to Control the Robot

Now that Flask is installed, we'll create a simple web server that provides a control panel with buttons to command the robot's movements. We'll set up routes in Flask to handle each movement command (forward, backward, left, right, and stop) and control the robot accordingly.

Step 1: Writing the Flask Web Server Code

1. Open a Terminal and create a new directory for the web server:

    bash

    ```
    mkdir ~/robot_web_interface
    cd ~/robot_web_interface
    ```

2. Create a new Python file for the web server:

    bash

    Copy code

    ```
    nano app.py
    ```

3. Write the following code to set up the Flask server and handle movement commands:

    python

    ```python
    from flask import Flask, render_template, request
    import RPi.GPIO as GPIO
    import time

    # Set up GPIO mode
    GPIO.setmode(GPIO.BCM)

    # Motor control pins
    ```

```python
IN1 = 18
IN2 = 23
IN3 = 24
IN4 = 25
ENA = 17
ENB = 27


# Set up motor pins
GPIO.setup(IN1, GPIO.OUT)
GPIO.setup(IN2, GPIO.OUT)
GPIO.setup(IN3, GPIO.OUT)
GPIO.setup(IN4, GPIO.OUT)
GPIO.setup(ENA, GPIO.OUT)
GPIO.setup(ENB, GPIO.OUT)


# Set up PWM on Enable pins
pwmA = GPIO.PWM(ENA, 100)
pwmB = GPIO.PWM(ENB, 100)
pwmA.start(50)  # Start with 50% speed
pwmB.start(50)  # Start with 50% speed


# Define movement functions
def move_forward():
    GPIO.output(IN1, GPIO.HIGH)
    GPIO.output(IN2, GPIO.LOW)
```

```python
    GPIO.output(IN3, GPIO.HIGH)
    GPIO.output(IN4, GPIO.LOW)

def move_backward():
    GPIO.output(IN1, GPIO.LOW)
    GPIO.output(IN2, GPIO.HIGH)
    GPIO.output(IN3, GPIO.LOW)
    GPIO.output(IN4, GPIO.HIGH)

def turn_left():
    GPIO.output(IN1, GPIO.LOW)
    GPIO.output(IN2, GPIO.LOW)
    GPIO.output(IN3, GPIO.HIGH)
    GPIO.output(IN4, GPIO.LOW)

def turn_right():
    GPIO.output(IN1, GPIO.HIGH)
    GPIO.output(IN2, GPIO.LOW)
    GPIO.output(IN3, GPIO.LOW)
    GPIO.output(IN4, GPIO.LOW)

def stop():
    GPIO.output(IN1, GPIO.LOW)
    GPIO.output(IN2, GPIO.LOW)
    GPIO.output(IN3, GPIO.LOW)
```

```python
        GPIO.output(IN4, GPIO.LOW)

    # Initialize Flask app
    app = Flask(__name__)

    # Define routes for each movement command
    @app.route('/')
    def index():
        return render_template('index.html')

    @app.route('/forward')
    def forward():
        move_forward()
        time.sleep(1)
        stop()
        return 'Moving Forward'

    @app.route('/backward')
    def backward():
        move_backward()
        time.sleep(1)
        stop()
        return 'Moving Backward'

    @app.route('/left')
```

```python
def left():
    turn_left()
    time.sleep(0.5)
    stop()
    return 'Turning Left'

@app.route('/right')
def right():
    turn_right()
    time.sleep(0.5)
    stop()
    return 'Turning Right'

@app.route('/stop')
def halt():
    stop()
    return 'Stopping'

if __name__ == '__main__':
    try:
        app.run(host='0.0.0.0', port=5000)
    finally:
        GPIO.cleanup()
```

4. Save and exit the file (**Ctrl + O**, **Enter**, then **Ctrl + X**).

ROBOTICS WITH RASPBERRY PI: BUILD YOUR FIRST ROBOT

Explanation of the Code:

- **Flask Routes**: Each route (e.g., /forward, /backward) corresponds to a movement command. When a button is clicked on the web interface, the robot performs the action for a specified duration, then stops.
- **Web Server Setup**: The Flask app is set to run on the IP address 0.0.0.0, making it accessible from any device on the same network.
- **GPIO Cleanup**: The program ensures GPIO is cleaned up after stopping the server.

Step 2: Creating the HTML Template for the Control Panel

1. Create a folder for templates:

   bash
   mkdir templates

2. Create an HTML file for the control panel:

   bash
   Copy code
   nano templates/index.html

3. Write the following HTML code for a simple web interface with movement buttons:

html

Copy code

```
<!DOCTYPE html>
<html lang="en">
<head>
  <meta charset="UTF-8">
  <meta name="viewport" content="width=device-width, initial-scale=1.0">
  <title>Robot Control Panel</title>
  <style>
    body { text-align: center; font-family: Arial, sans-serif; }
    button { font-size: 20px; padding: 10px 20px; margin: 10px; }
  </style>
</head>
<body>
  <h1>Robot Control Panel</h1>
  <button onclick="fetch('/forward')">Forward</button><br>
  <button onclick="fetch('/left')">Left</button>
  <button onclick="fetch('/stop')">Stop</button>
  <button onclick="fetch('/right')">Right</button><br>
  <button onclick="fetch('/backward')">Backward</button>
```

```
</body>
</html>
```

4. Save and exit the file.

Explanation of the HTML Code:

- **JavaScript Fetch Calls**: Each button uses JavaScript's fetch function to send a request to the corresponding route (e.g., /forward for forward movement).
- **Control Panel Layout**: The control panel has buttons for each movement direction and a "Stop" button in the center.

Running the Web Server

1. In the Terminal, start the Flask web server:

bash
```
python3 app.py
```

2. **Accessing the Control Panel**:
   o Open a web browser on any device connected to the same Wi-Fi network.
   o Enter the IP address and port in the address bar (e.g., http://192.168.1.100:5000).
   o You should see the control panel interface with buttons for controlling the robot.

3. **Testing the Controls**:

   o Click the "Forward" button and observe the robot moving forward.

   o Use the "Left," "Right," and "Backward" buttons to control the direction.

   o Press "Stop" to halt the robot.

Expanding the Web Interface Capabilities

Once you have a basic control panel, consider expanding it with additional features:

1. **Speed Control**: Add buttons to increase or decrease motor speed using PWM.

2. **Real-time Video Feed**: Embed a live video stream from the camera so you can see the robot's environment remotely.

3. **Status Display**: Show the robot's current status (e.g., battery level, distance to obstacles).

In this chapter, you learned to set up Wi-Fi on the Raspberry Pi, build a simple web interface using Flask, and control your robot over a local network. By hosting a Flask web server and creating a web-based control panel, you made your robot accessible from any device with a browser.

In the next chapter, we'll explore integrating real-time data from sensors into the web interface, allowing you to monitor the robot's surroundings and make more informed control decisions remotely. This will further enhance the robot's interactivity and functionality.

CHAPTER 20: AUTONOMOUS NAVIGATION WITH SENSORS AND MAPPING

Autonomous navigation enables a robot to move through an environment without manual control, relying on sensors and mapping to make decisions. This chapter introduces the key concepts in autonomous navigation and mapping, explains how to use sensor data to create a basic map of the robot's surroundings, and provides hands-on steps to program your robot to navigate a small area independently. By the end of this chapter, your robot will have the foundation to make its way through a space autonomously.

Concepts in Autonomous Navigation and Mapping

Autonomous navigation is essential in robotics, allowing a robot to perceive and interact with its environment. Navigation involves three main concepts:

1. **Perception**: Gathering data about the environment using sensors such as ultrasonic sensors, infrared (IR) sensors, or

LiDAR to detect obstacles, measure distances, and identify free paths.

2. **Mapping**: Using sensor data to create a representation (map) of the environment, enabling the robot to remember obstacle locations and plan routes.

3. **Path Planning**: Determining the best path to reach a destination while avoiding obstacles. Basic path planning includes identifying open areas and avoiding known obstacles.

Types of Maps in Robotics:

- **Grid Maps**: A grid-based map divides the space into cells, with each cell representing either free space, an obstacle, or an unknown area.

- **Occupancy Grids**: Each cell in an occupancy grid has a probability representing the likelihood of it being occupied. These are commonly used in autonomous navigation to manage uncertain environments.

- **Feature Maps**: Instead of grids, feature maps track specific landmarks, such as walls or large objects, providing a less granular but memory-efficient representation.

In this chapter, we'll focus on a simple **grid map** that allows the robot to mark free spaces and obstacles as it explores.

Using Sensor Data to Create a Basic Map of the Robot's Environment

To create a basic map, we'll use ultrasonic sensors to detect obstacles and build a simple grid-based representation of the environment. As the robot moves, it will record data from the sensors and mark each grid cell as "occupied" or "free."

Materials Needed:

- Ultrasonic sensors or IR sensors for obstacle detection
- A pre-defined area (e.g., 1m x 1m) with marked boundaries to navigate

Grid Setup:

- For simplicity, divide the robot's environment into a grid (e.g., a 5x5 grid representing a 1m x 1m area).
- Each grid cell will store a value indicating whether it is free (0) or occupied by an obstacle (1).

Example Grid:

plaintext

Copy code

```
0 0 0 1 0
0 1 0 1 0
0 0 0 0 0
1 0 1 0 0
```

0 0 0 1 1

Each cell represents a section of the area, and the robot updates this grid based on sensor feedback as it moves.

Hands-on: Programming Your Robot to Navigate a Small Area Autonomously

In this hands-on section, we'll write code to:

1. Move the robot through a grid-based area.
2. Use sensor data to detect obstacles.
3. Update the grid map with detected obstacles.

Step 1: Writing the Autonomous Navigation Code

1. Open a Terminal on the Raspberry Pi and create a new Python file:

   bash

   nano autonomous_navigation.py

2. Write the following code to implement grid-based navigation and mapping:

   python
   import RPi.GPIO as GPIO
   import time

   # Set up GPIO mode

```python
GPIO.setmode(GPIO.BCM)

# Motor control pins
IN1 = 18
IN2 = 23
IN3 = 24
IN4 = 25
ENA = 17
ENB = 27

# Set up motor pins
GPIO.setup(IN1, GPIO.OUT)
GPIO.setup(IN2, GPIO.OUT)
GPIO.setup(IN3, GPIO.OUT)
GPIO.setup(IN4, GPIO.OUT)
GPIO.setup(ENA, GPIO.OUT)
GPIO.setup(ENB, GPIO.OUT)

# Set up PWM on Enable pins
pwmA = GPIO.PWM(ENA, 100)
pwmB = GPIO.PWM(ENB, 100)
pwmA.start(50)  # Start with 50% speed
pwmB.start(50)  # Start with 50% speed

# Ultrasonic sensor pins
```

```
TRIG = 20
ECHO = 21

GPIO.setup(TRIG, GPIO.OUT)
GPIO.setup(ECHO, GPIO.IN)

# Define movement functions
def move_forward():
    GPIO.output(IN1, GPIO.HIGH)
    GPIO.output(IN2, GPIO.LOW)
    GPIO.output(IN3, GPIO.HIGH)
    GPIO.output(IN4, GPIO.LOW)
    time.sleep(0.5)

def turn_left():
    GPIO.output(IN1, GPIO.LOW)
    GPIO.output(IN2, GPIO.LOW)
    GPIO.output(IN3, GPIO.HIGH)
    GPIO.output(IN4, GPIO.LOW)
    time.sleep(0.5)

def turn_right():
    GPIO.output(IN1, GPIO.HIGH)
    GPIO.output(IN2, GPIO.LOW)
    GPIO.output(IN3, GPIO.LOW)
```

```python
        GPIO.output(IN4, GPIO.LOW)
        time.sleep(0.5)

def stop():
        GPIO.output(IN1, GPIO.LOW)
        GPIO.output(IN2, GPIO.LOW)
        GPIO.output(IN3, GPIO.LOW)
        GPIO.output(IN4, GPIO.LOW)

# Function to measure distance
def measure_distance():
        GPIO.output(TRIG, True)
        time.sleep(0.00001)
        GPIO.output(TRIG, False)

        start_time = time.time()
        stop_time = time.time()

        while GPIO.input(ECHO) == 0:
            start_time = time.time()

        while GPIO.input(ECHO) == 1:
            stop_time = time.time()

        elapsed_time = stop_time - start_time
```

```python
    distance = (elapsed_time * 34300) / 2  # Speed of sound
in cm/s
    return distance


# Initialize a 5x5 grid map (0 = free, 1 = occupied)
grid_size = 5
grid_map = [[0 for _ in range(grid_size)] for _ in
range(grid_size)]
robot_position = [2, 2]  # Starting at the center of the grid


# Update the map with obstacles based on sensor readings
def update_map():
    distance = measure_distance()
    if distance < 20:  # Obstacle detected within 20 cm
        x, y = robot_position
        grid_map[y][x] = 1    # Mark the current cell as
occupied
        print("Obstacle detected at position:", robot_position)


# Display the grid map
def display_map():
    for row in grid_map:
        print(" ".join(str(cell) for cell in row))


# Main loop for autonomous navigation
```

```
try:
    for _ in range(10):  # Move for 10 steps
        update_map()  # Update map based on sensor readings

        # Basic navigation logic
        if  grid_map[robot_position[1]][robot_position[0]]  ==
1:
            turn_right()  # Turn right if an obstacle is detected
        else:
            move_forward()   # Move forward if no obstacle
detected
        # Update robot position in the grid
        robot_position[1] += 1

        stop()  # Stop briefly to take measurements
        display_map()  # Print the updated map

finally:
    stop()
    GPIO.cleanup()
    print("GPIO cleaned up")
```

3. Save and exit the file (**Ctrl + O, Enter,** then **Ctrl + X**).

Explanation of the Code:

- **Grid Map**: The grid_map is a 5x5 matrix representing the environment. Cells are updated as "free" or "occupied" based on sensor readings.
- **Movement Logic**: The robot moves forward unless an obstacle is detected within 20 cm, in which case it turns right.
- **Map Display**: After each step, the program prints the current map to show detected obstacles.

Running the Autonomous Navigation Program

1. Run the program with:

bash

python3 autonomous_navigation.py

2. **Testing Navigation and Mapping**:
   - Observe the robot as it navigates the environment. Each time an obstacle is detected, it should turn and update the map.
   - The grid map printed to the terminal will display the robot's perception of the environment, with obstacles marked as 1.

3. **Analyzing the Map Output**:

o After the robot completes its steps, the printed map will show where it encountered obstacles, giving a basic representation of the environment.

Expanding Autonomous Navigation Capabilities

Once you've implemented basic navigation, consider expanding this functionality:

1. **Path Planning**: Implement path-planning algorithms (e.g., A* algorithm) to navigate around obstacles and reach a specified target.
2. **Multiple Sensors**: Add more sensors to detect obstacles from the sides and enhance the robot's perception.
3. **Dynamic Mapping**: Update the map continuously as the robot moves to create a more detailed and accurate representation of the environment.

In this chapter, you learned the fundamentals of autonomous navigation and mapping, used sensor data to create a basic grid map of the environment, and programmed your robot to navigate a small area autonomously. This foundation in navigation is crucial for building fully autonomous robots capable of exploring, mapping, and moving within complex environments.

In the next chapter, we'll dive deeper into path planning and more advanced mapping techniques, enhancing the robot's ability to move intelligently and reach specific destinations within its mapped environment.

Chapter 21: Testing, Debugging, and Optimization

Testing, debugging, and optimization are essential for creating a reliable and efficient robot. In this chapter, we'll discuss common issues in Raspberry Pi robotics, go over debugging techniques, and share tips for testing and refining the robot's movements, sensor accuracy, and responsiveness. We'll also cover optimization strategies to improve the robot's performance and reliability, ensuring it operates smoothly in various environments.

Common Issues and Debugging Techniques in Raspberry Pi Robotics

Robotics projects often encounter a variety of issues, including hardware malfunctions, software bugs, and integration problems.

Here are some of the most common issues in Raspberry Pi robotics and techniques to address them:

1. **Power Issues**:
   o **Symptom**: The robot behaves unpredictably, resets randomly, or the motors slow down when other components are active.
   o **Solution**: Use a reliable power supply, ideally with separate power sources for the Raspberry Pi and motors to avoid power drain. Battery packs or power banks can provide stable power for both the Raspberry Pi and motors.

2. **GPIO and Wiring Errors**:
   o **Symptom**: Motors don't turn on, sensors give no readings, or components behave erratically.
   o **Solution**: Double-check wiring connections and pin assignments. Ensure that all components are correctly grounded and that GPIO pins match those specified in the code.

3. **Sensor Malfunction**:
   o **Symptom**: Sensors give inconsistent readings, fail to detect obstacles, or show constant values.
   o **Solution**: Verify sensor positioning and alignment. Use test scripts to read sensor values individually, checking the range and consistency of readings.

Clean sensor lenses, especially for ultrasonic or IR sensors, as dust or obstructions can impact accuracy.

4. **Code Errors**:

   o **Symptom**: The robot doesn't perform expected actions, errors appear in the terminal, or the program crashes.

   o **Solution**: Use error handling, print statements, and debugging tools like pdb to track variable states and identify issues. Break down the code into smaller functions and test each one individually to pinpoint problems.

Debugging Techniques:

- **Print Statements**: Add print statements to display values of critical variables, helping you understand the code flow and detect unexpected behaviors.

- **Error Handling**: Wrap code blocks in try/except statements to catch errors and print informative messages when something goes wrong.

- **Sensor Calibration**: Regularly calibrate sensors, especially distance sensors and encoders, to ensure accurate readings. Test sensors individually to ensure they are functioning correctly.

Testing and Refining Movement, Sensor Accuracy, and Responsiveness

Once the robot is operational, thorough testing helps ensure that it performs reliably. Focus on key aspects like movement, sensor accuracy, and overall responsiveness.

1. Movement Testing and Calibration:

- **Straight-Line Movement**: Run the robot in a straight line and observe any drift to the left or right. Adjust motor speeds or PWM values to correct any imbalance.
- **Turning Radius**: Test turns to ensure they're consistent. If turns are too sharp or too wide, adjust the turn timing or motor speed.
- **Speed Control**: Use PWM (pulse-width modulation) to adjust motor speeds. Experiment with different PWM values to achieve smooth acceleration and deceleration.

2. Sensor Testing and Calibration:

- **Distance Accuracy**: Measure the accuracy of distance sensors by comparing sensor readings with actual measurements. Adjust threshold values in the code to improve detection reliability.
- **Obstacle Detection**: Test obstacle detection by placing objects at various distances and angles. Confirm that the

robot responds to obstacles appropriately and updates its map correctly.

- **Environmental Sensitivity**: Some sensors, like IR, can be affected by lighting conditions. Test in different lighting environments and consider alternatives, like ultrasonic sensors, if IR accuracy varies significantly.

3. Responsiveness:

- **Command Latency**: Test the response time between issuing a command and the robot's action. If there's noticeable lag, check for delays in the code or network connectivity issues if using remote control.
- **Real-Time Feedback**: For autonomous behavior, ensure sensors are read frequently enough to allow timely reactions. Adjust the time.sleep() intervals in the code to balance processing speed and responsiveness.

Practical Tips to Improve Your Robot's Performance and Reliability

Improving the performance and reliability of your robot involves fine-tuning both the hardware setup and the software logic. Here are some practical tips to enhance overall performance:

1. **Optimize Power Management**:

- Use separate power supplies for the Raspberry Pi and motors to prevent power dips and improve stability.
- Consider using power management ICs or battery packs with voltage regulation to ensure consistent voltage output, especially for extended operation.

2. **Refine Code Efficiency**:
   - **Reduce Delay**: Limit the use of time.sleep() in critical control loops, especially in real-time applications like obstacle detection and navigation.
   - **Optimize Sensor Polling**: Use conditional checks or interrupts (where possible) to read sensor data only when necessary, reducing processor load.
   - **Minimize Computation**: In navigation routines, simplify calculations when possible to avoid unnecessary processing delays.

3. **Modularize the Code**:
   - Break the code into functions or modules for each subsystem (movement, obstacle detection, mapping, etc.). This makes it easier to debug and test each function independently.
   - Encapsulate functions like move_forward() and measure_distance() in separate files if your codebase becomes large, improving readability and maintainability.

4. **Calibrate Regularly**:

   o Sensor accuracy can drift over time, especially in changing environmental conditions. Periodic calibration ensures sensors provide reliable readings, which is critical for autonomous behavior.

   o Calibration routines can also be added to the program, allowing the robot to recalibrate at startup or in response to specific commands.

5. **Reduce Physical Wear and Tear**:

   o Inspect the robot's hardware periodically to check for loose connections, worn-out wheels, or motor issues.

   o Ensure wiring and connectors are secure, as vibrations from movement can loosen connections over time.

6. **Logging and Monitoring**:

   o Add logging functions to record sensor data and actions. This helps diagnose performance issues and understand how the robot behaves in different scenarios.

   o For real-time monitoring, consider displaying data on a web interface or sending it to an external system for logging, which can help with troubleshooting during testing.

7. **Implement Safety Mechanisms**:

- o Program emergency stop conditions if the robot detects an unknown error or loses connectivity.
- o Add boundary detection if your robot operates in a specific area, stopping or turning the robot if it reaches the edge of the allowed space.

Sample Testing Script for Movement and Sensor Accuracy

Here's a simple script that tests the robot's movement and sensor accuracy, providing printouts for each step to ensure the robot is functioning as expected:

1. Open a Terminal on the Raspberry Pi and create a new file:

```bash
nano test_robot.py
```

2. Write the following code to test forward movement, turning, and sensor distance measurements:

```python
import RPi.GPIO as GPIO
import time

# Motor control pins and setup
IN1 = 18
IN2 = 23
IN3 = 24
```

```python
IN4 = 25
ENA = 17
ENB = 27

GPIO.setmode(GPIO.BCM)
GPIO.setup(IN1, GPIO.OUT)
GPIO.setup(IN2, GPIO.OUT)
GPIO.setup(IN3, GPIO.OUT)
GPIO.setup(IN4, GPIO.OUT)
GPIO.setup(ENA, GPIO.OUT)
GPIO.setup(ENB, GPIO.OUT)

pwmA = GPIO.PWM(ENA, 100)
pwmB = GPIO.PWM(ENB, 100)
pwmA.start(50)
pwmB.start(50)

# Ultrasonic sensor setup
TRIG = 20
ECHO = 21
GPIO.setup(TRIG, GPIO.OUT)
GPIO.setup(ECHO, GPIO.IN)

def move_forward():
    print("Moving forward")
```

```python
    GPIO.output(IN1, GPIO.HIGH)
    GPIO.output(IN2, GPIO.LOW)
    GPIO.output(IN3, GPIO.HIGH)
    GPIO.output(IN4, GPIO.LOW)
    time.sleep(1)
    stop()

def turn_left():
    print("Turning left")
    GPIO.output(IN1, GPIO.LOW)
    GPIO.output(IN2, GPIO.LOW)
    GPIO.output(IN3, GPIO.HIGH)
    GPIO.output(IN4, GPIO.LOW)
    time.sleep(0.5)
    stop()

def stop():
    GPIO.output(IN1, GPIO.LOW)
    GPIO.output(IN2, GPIO.LOW)
    GPIO.output(IN3, GPIO.LOW)
    GPIO.output(IN4, GPIO.LOW)

def measure_distance():
    GPIO.output(TRIG, True)
    time.sleep(0.00001)
```

```
    GPIO.output(TRIG, False)
    start_time = time.time()
    stop_time = time.time()

    while GPIO.input(ECHO) == 0:
        start_time = time.time()

    while GPIO.input(ECHO) == 1:
        stop_time = time.time()

    elapsed_time = stop_time - start_time
    distance = (elapsed_time * 34300) / 2
    print(f"Distance: {distance:.2f} cm")
    return distance

try:
    print("Starting movement and sensor tests...")
    move_forward()
    turn_left()
    distance = measure_distance()

    if distance < 20:
        print("Obstacle detected within 20 cm")

finally:
```

```
stop()
GPIO.cleanup()
print("GPIO cleaned up")
```

3. Save and run the script:

```
bash
python3 test_robot.py
```

This script provides a basic test of movement functions and the ultrasonic sensor, helping to identify any issues before moving on to more complex tasks.

In this chapter, you learned about common issues and debugging techniques in Raspberry Pi robotics, tested and refined the robot's movement and sensor accuracy, and applied optimization strategies to improve performance and reliability. These steps are essential to ensure your robot functions consistently and can handle various environments and tasks.

In the final chapter, we'll discuss deployment and maintenance, covering strategies to keep your robot operational over time, including regular testing, maintenance routines, and potential upgrades to expand functionality.

CHAPTER 22: SHOWCASING AND EXPANDING YOUR ROBOT

With your robot now operational and optimized, it's time to consider how to showcase it effectively and think about expanding its capabilities for future projects. In this chapter, we'll cover best practices for preparing your robot for demonstrations or project showcases, provide tips for documenting and sharing your work, and explore ideas for enhancing your robot with advanced features.

Preparing Your Robot for a Demonstration or Project Showcase

A well-prepared demonstration not only highlights your robot's capabilities but also communicates the effort and thought behind your work. Here are key steps to prepare your robot for a successful showcase:

1. **Define the Purpose of the Demonstration**:
   - Decide on the key features you want to showcase. Is it autonomous navigation, object tracking, or remote control? Tailoring the demonstration to highlight specific capabilities ensures a focused presentation.
   - Outline the sequence of actions your robot will perform during the demo. For example, if you're showcasing navigation, plan a path with obstacles to show the robot's ability to avoid them.

2. **Test and Troubleshoot in Advance**:
   - Conduct multiple test runs in the demonstration space to ensure the robot performs as expected in the given environment. This is particularly important if lighting or floor texture differs from your testing area.
   - Prepare for potential issues by checking power sources, confirming stable connections, and inspecting sensors and motors for functionality.

3. **Prepare a Backup Plan**:

- Sometimes, things don't go as planned. Prepare a backup script or pre-recorded video of the robot in action in case of unexpected technical issues. This allows you to still demonstrate your work even if live functionality fails.

4. **Explain Key Features and Technical Details**:
   - Prepare a brief overview of your robot's design, key features, and underlying technology. Use visuals like diagrams or photos to illustrate the robot's components, wiring, and coding structure.
   - Be ready to answer questions about the robot's sensors, code, and any algorithms used, especially if presenting to a technical audience.

5. **Clean and Aesthetic Presentation**:
   - Ensure your robot is clean, with wires neatly organized and components firmly attached. A tidy setup makes the robot look more professional and easier for the audience to understand.
   - Use labels or a poster board with diagrams to explain each component's function, helping viewers quickly grasp how your robot works.

Tips for Documenting Your Robot Project and Sharing It with Others

Documentation is essential to showcase your project, whether for a presentation, portfolio, or online community. Here's how to document your robot effectively:

1. **Create a Project Overview**:
   - Start with a high-level description of your project, including its purpose, features, and goals. Explain why you built this robot and what unique functionalities it has.

2. **Include Technical Details**:
   - Detail the hardware and software used, including the Raspberry Pi model, sensors, motors, power sources, and libraries. Include a parts list for easy reference.
   - Explain key algorithms or techniques you implemented, such as obstacle avoidance, object tracking, or voice control. Diagrams and pseudo-code can help illustrate complex processes.

3. **Step-by-Step Instructions**:
   - Document each step of your build process, from assembling the hardware to programming the robot. Include setup and installation instructions for dependencies, libraries, or other software requirements.
   - Capture photos and screenshots of each stage to create a visual guide. This is especially helpful if

you plan to share your project as an educational resource.

4. **Record Performance Metrics**:

   o Include data on how your robot performs, such as average speed, obstacle detection range, and battery life. These metrics provide insights into the robot's capabilities and help others replicate or build upon your work.

5. **Highlight Challenges and Solutions**:

   o Document any major challenges you faced and how you overcame them. This can include debugging issues, design modifications, or algorithm adjustments. Sharing problem-solving strategies adds value to your project and demonstrates critical thinking.

6. **Create a Demonstration Video**:

   o A video is one of the most effective ways to showcase your project. Record the robot performing key actions, explain its features as it runs, and include close-ups of the robot's components.

   o Narrate or add captions to guide viewers through each feature, making it easy to understand even for those unfamiliar with robotics.

7. **Share Your Project Online**:

- o Consider sharing your project on platforms like GitHub, Hackster.io, or robotics forums. Provide access to your code and instructions to help others learn from or replicate your work.
- o Engage with the community by responding to questions and sharing updates or improvements to your robot.

Ideas for Expanding Your Robot: Adding Advanced Sensors, More Autonomy, or New Features

Once your robot is complete, you may want to enhance it further by adding advanced features. Here are some ideas for expanding its capabilities:

1. **Advanced Sensors and Modules**:
   - o **LiDAR or Depth Sensors**: Add a LiDAR or depth sensor for more precise mapping and obstacle detection. These sensors can significantly improve navigation in complex environments.
   - o **GPS Module**: If you want to take your robot outdoors, a GPS module can help it navigate larger areas by plotting waypoints.
   - o **Temperature and Humidity Sensors**: Add environmental sensors to monitor and respond to temperature or humidity, useful for robotics applications in weather monitoring or agriculture.

2. **Increased Autonomy**:

   o **Path Planning Algorithms**: Implement algorithms like A* or Dijkstra's for complex path planning. This allows your robot to find optimal routes and avoid obstacles intelligently.

   o **Simultaneous Localization and Mapping (SLAM)**: For more advanced projects, consider implementing SLAM. This technique allows the robot to map an environment while simultaneously tracking its position, which is useful in unknown environments.

   o **Machine Learning for Object Recognition**: Add a trained object recognition model to enable your robot to identify specific objects or people. This can allow it to interact dynamically with its surroundings, recognizing objects and responding accordingly.

3. **Enhanced Interaction and Control**:

   o **Gesture Recognition**: Use a camera and machine learning model to enable gesture recognition. This can allow users to control the robot using hand signals.

   o **Voice Commands**: Expand voice control by integrating more advanced speech recognition and natural language processing (NLP), enabling the robot to understand more complex commands or engage in simple conversations.

- o **Multi-Device Control**: Set up a web interface that allows multiple users to control or monitor the robot simultaneously, useful for team-based demonstrations or remote interactions.

4. **New Functionalities and Applications**:

- o **Line Following**: Implement line-following capabilities to enable your robot to follow marked paths. This can be especially useful in warehouse or industrial applications.

- o **Object Manipulation**: Add a robotic arm or gripper to give your robot the ability to pick up, move, or interact with objects. This opens up applications in automation or material handling.

- o **Data Logging and Analytics**: Program the robot to log data during operation, such as sensor readings, movement patterns, and battery levels. Use this data for analytics or machine learning to improve performance over time.

5. **Connectivity and IoT Integration**:

- o **IoT Platform Integration**: Connect your robot to an IoT platform like AWS IoT, Google Cloud IoT, or ThingSpeak. This enables remote monitoring, control, and data analytics.

- o **Cloud Processing for AI**: Offload intensive tasks, like image recognition or natural language processing, to the cloud. This approach can significantly enhance the robot's capabilities while reducing the load on the Raspberry Pi.
- o **Mobile App Control**: Develop a mobile app to control your robot and monitor its status in real-time. This adds convenience and accessibility for users.

6. **Build for Specific Applications**:
  - o **Surveillance Robot**: Add a camera with live streaming, remote control, and motion detection to turn your robot into a mobile surveillance system.
  - o **Delivery or Transportation Robot**: Equip the robot with a small platform or tray to transport items. This can be adapted for home assistance, office deliveries, or inventory management.
  - o **Educational or Social Robot**: Program the robot to engage with users through voice, gestures, or even games. This is ideal for interactive educational purposes or as a social companion.

Showcasing Your Expanded Project

As you expand your robot, document new features, and demonstrate advanced functionalities to showcase your continuous progress. Consider creating a project roadmap that shows how your robot has evolved, which helps others understand the developmental stages and inspires them to try similar expansions.

1. **Keep a Development Log**:
   - o Record each new feature you add and its purpose. Include code snippets, photos, and explanations of design decisions.
   - o Document any challenges encountered during expansion and the solutions you used, which can provide valuable insights for future projects or for others replicating your work.

2. **Share Updates with the Community**:
   - o Update your project on GitHub, social media, or online robotics communities to showcase the latest improvements.
   - o If your robot is particularly unique or complex, consider writing a blog post, article, or tutorial to share the details.

3. **Present Expanded Capabilities in Demonstrations**:
   - o When showcasing new features, walk the audience through each new capability, explaining how it improves the robot's functionality.
   - o Include examples or applications for each new feature to illustrate practical use cases.

In this final chapter, you learned how to prepare your robot for demonstrations, document your project for sharing, and brainstorm ways to expand its capabilities. By organizing, presenting, and sharing your work effectively, you help others learn from your experience while showcasing your skills and creativity.

This guide has taken you from the basics of building a Raspberry Pi-powered robot to advanced functionality and potential expansions. With a strong foundation, you're now ready to take on more ambitious robotics projects, explore cutting-edge technology, and continually improve your skills. Good luck, and keep innovating!

www.ingramcontent.com/pod-product-compliance
Lightning Source LLC
Chambersburg PA
CBHW071240050326
40690CB00011B/2198

* 9 7 9 8 3 4 5 3 5 8 7 0 2 *